ISSUES THAT CONCERN YOU

Discrimination

Lauri S. Friedman, *Book Editor*

Christine Nasso, *Publisher*
Elizabeth Des Chenes, *Managing Editor*

D0605022

GREENHAVEN PRESS
An imprint of Thomson Gale, a part of The Thomson Corporation

THOMSON
™
GALE

Detroit • New York • San Francisco • New Haven, Conn. • Waterville, Maine • London

LIBRARY OF CONGRESS CATALOGING-IN-PUBLICATION DATA
Discrimination / Lauri S. Friedman, book editor.
p. cm. — (Issues that concern you)
Includes bibliographical references and index.
ISBN-13: 978-0-7377-3813-1 (hardcover)
1. Discrimination—United States. I. Friedman, Lauri S.
HN90.S6D57 2008
305.0973—dc22
2007037477

ISBN-10: 0-7377-3813-8
Printed in the United States of America

CONTENTS

Discrimination comes in a myriad of forms, against innumerable types of people. Discrimination goes far beyond racial or ethnic prejudice (though discrimination based on race and ethnicity is a common form of the practice). People can be discriminated against because of their age—employers have been sued because of their reluctance to hire a person who is older, believing they are out of touch with industry innovations. People can also be discriminated against if they have a disability, both in the workplace and in society. Sexual orientation, religion, and national origin are other qualifiers that have provoked unjust discrimination throughout the ages.

But one of the most enduring forms of discrimination is that based on gender, usually the discrimination of women in the workplace. When people discuss the discrimination of women in the workplace, they often focus on the wage gap—that is, the fact that women are on average paid less than men. Indeed, the unequal pay of women has been a problem for decades, causing Congress in 1963 to pass the Equal Pay Act, which requires that men and women be given equal pay for equal work in the same establishment. In 1963 women earned about 59 percent of the wages men earned. The pay gap has narrowed since then thanks in part to the Equal Pay Act, but still exists. As of 2007 American women continue to earn on average less than American men. According to the U.S. Census Bureau, women are paid approximately 77 cents for every dollar a man is paid. Economist Evelyn Murphy, president and founder of the WAGE Project, which tracks the differences of pay between men and women, estimates the wage gap costs the average full-time U.S. woman worker between $700,000 and $2 million over the course of her work life.

Women of color suffer from the wage gap even more—it is reported that African American women earn only 68 cents and Latinas 57 cents for every dollar that men earn. Asian American and Pacific Islander American women are statistically the best earners of all women, but still earn only 88 cents for every dollar that men earn. Perhaps most alarmingly, the pay gap is not a remnant of past inequalities in which women were educated less than men. For more than 25 years women have accounted for the majority of the nation's college students (with 58 percent of college students women, and just 42 percent men in 2006). And a 2007 study by the American Association of University Women found that even just one year after college graduation, women earn only 80 percent of what men do. That gap continues to widen over time. In America, Louisiana has the biggest pay disparity; there, college-educated women over twenty-five earn 64 percent of what their male counterparts do. Women in West Virginia and Washington, D.C., earn more, but still less than their male counterparts, at 89 percent of what men earn.

Demonstrators rally in York, Pennyslvania, to express their support for diversity.

That a persistent and ongoing gap exists between men and women's wages is undisputed. What is of more controversy, however, is whether discrimination is the cause of the gap in pay. Some argue that discrimination is in fact the culprit. Indeed, the assumption that men can outperform women in certain fields and a preference to promote men rather than women continue. Female job applicants are at a disadvantage when they have children or are of child bearing age, as employers may be unwilling to hire someone who is likely to go on maternity leave. Finally, women suffer discrimination in the perception that they are less deserving of the same working conditions as men. For example, after studying the treatment of female and male employees, the Massachusetts Institute of Technology found that its female scientists were routinely given less pay, space, funding, and rewards than their male colleagues. "Did anyone intentionally give them smaller offices and labs? Probably not. It's just one of those things [that] accumulate and add up to barriers and institutional discrimination," said Heidi Hartmann, president of the Institute for Women's Policy Research.

Others argue that overt discrimination explains only part of the ongoing wage gap, and they suggest that other nondiscriminatory factors are responsible for men and women's salaries continuing to be unequal. One such explanation is that women tend to avoid negotiating—and negotiating is key to increasing a person's salary. According to *Women Don't Ask: Negotiation and the Gender Divide* by Linda Babcock and Sara Laschever, men initiate negotiations four times more often than women do. Negotiating is unpleasant for many women: When asked to compare negotiating to another task, Babcock and Laschever found that men likened negotiating to "winning a ballgame" or a "wrestling match." Women, on the other hand, compared negotiating to "going to the dentist." Furthermore, women tend to underestimate the amount of money available for negotiations. Consequently, when they do negotiate, they typically ask for and thus get less—on average about 30 percent less than men. Babcock and Laschever explain that women's dislike of negotiating hurts them substantially; over the course of a person's working life, they estimate, an individual stands to lose more than $500,000 by not negotiating his or her salary.

Yet another explanation for the wage gap is that the lifestyle goals of men and women cause them to earn different amounts. Warren Farrell, the author of *Why Men Earn More: The Startling Truth Behind the Pay Gap—and What Women Can Do About It*, found that men are more likely to sign up for tasks that directly increase their paycheck, such as relocating or traveling extensively for work; taking on dangerous or hazardous assignments; taking on jobs that involve greater financial risk; and working under unpleasant conditions (for example, in prisons or coal mines). Farrell and others also point out that women tend to earn less than men over the course of their careers because of their decision to drop out of the work force in order to raise children. Though the fact that women remain the primary caregivers to children may be the result of unfair or antiquated understanding of gender responsibilities, it is not a result of discrimination. As author Steve Chapman writes,

> The divergent career paths of men and women may reflect a basic unfairness in what's expected of them. It could be that a lot of mothers, if they had their way, would rather pursue careers but have to stay home with the kids because their husbands insist. Or it may be that for one reason or another, many mothers prefer to take on the lion's share of child-rearing. In any case, the pay disparity caused by these choices can't be blamed on piggish employers.

That American women continue to earn less than American men is just one issue relating to discrimination that will continue to be debated in the twenty-first century. It is also just one of the issues explored in *Issues That Concern You: Discrimination*. Readers will examine other forms of discrimination, such as racial, ethnic, religious, and sexual orientation discrimination and conclude for themselves whether discrimination continues to be a serious problem and whether or not certain behaviors qualify as discrimination.

ONE

Discrimination Against African Americans Is Still a Problem

Lewis W. Diuguid

Discrimination of African Americans is not yet a thing of the past, explains author Lewis W. Diuguid in the following essay. Diuguid recounts the story of eighteen-year-old Jumoke Balogun, who experienced racism in a McDonald's restaurant. A cashier refused to serve her food she paid for, while other customers muttered racial slurs as she left the restaurant. Although the incident is not earth-shattering, Diuguid argues it is proof that racism and discrimination continue to exist in American society. Compounding the situation is that young Americans do not have the tools to cope with discrimination the way their parents, many of whom grew up in an era characterized by overt racism, do. Diuguid concludes that the best way to work toward eradicating discrimination is to publicize incidents like Balogun's and demand better of society. Diuguid is vice president and columnist at the *Kansas City Star*, from which this viewpoint was taken.

Turning 18 years old and getting to vote this year had stood out as the biggest things in Jumoke Balogun's life.

But Balogun faced another major event in her life. It occurred at a McDonald's restaurant in Cass County. On Dec. 28 [2005], she and a friend went to McDonald's about 7 P.M. after shopping at a Target store. Her friend ordered a salad, and Balogun got a McChicken, fries and an apple pie.

A special at the restaurant ensured that she'd get two apple pies. The clerk behind the counter got her friend's order right, but she failed to give Balogun the second apple pie.

Publicly Embarrassed

Balogun pointed that out to the clerk, who was white and in her late 30s. The woman disputed her claim. Balogun produced the receipt. The clerk got the other apple pie, "slammed it on the counter and slid it toward me."

"She said, 'Merry Christmas,'" Balogun said. Other people were waiting in line, and Balogun was the only African-American in the place. "I was very embarrassed.

"I was kind of mad after that, but I wasn't as mad as I was hurt," Balogun said. She and her friend talked, but her friend didn't understand what had just happened.

"I thought it was racially motivated," said Balogun. "She thought the lady was rude and overworked."

"I Felt Small and Very Alone"

Balogun's friend said that if Balogun felt uncomfortable they should leave and eat their dinner in the car. "I wanted to cry," Balogun said.

"We were getting our food to leave," she said. "I didn't want to eat there at all. As we were leaving I heard a guy say the N-word.

"I know it was directed toward me. I looked down. I felt very, very bad.

"I didn't want the food anymore. We just left. I just wanted to get out of there as soon as possible. I was very, very uncomfortable.

"I felt really scared. I felt very small and alone. I still feel angry. That really never happened to me before."

She said she had never been followed in a shopping center because of racial profiling and never felt discriminated against. Only one other time when she was in fourth grade had a boy, who was white, used the N-word toward her, and that was at George Washington Carver Elementary School.

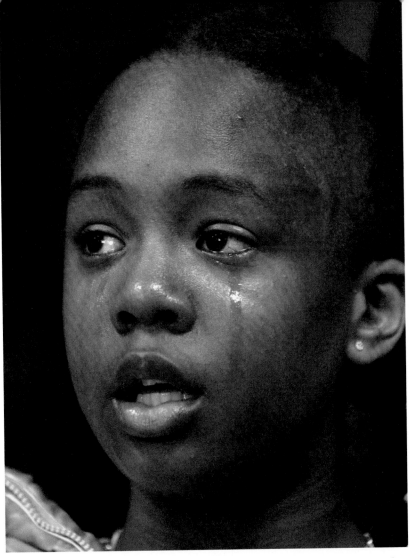

Jailana Leonard cries during a 2004 news conference. She and several other students in the Kent School District in Washington State sued the school claiming they were subjected to racist harassment by security guards.

Small Incidents Equal Big Trouble

Balogun, who was a high school friend of my daughter's, shared her story in January at the All Souls Unitarian Universalist Church on "Dr. Martin L. King Jr.'s Legacy: Visions from a New Generation."

It's important to share Balogun's impressions during this 30th anniversary of Black History Month because what she endured says a lot about this area's ongoing problems with race. I worry about millennials like her. They are African-Americans who are my children's age.

Many grow up now unschooled by Jim Crow. The best of America's bigotry was good at teaching preschool to college lessons in racism and discrimination to my generation and those before me.

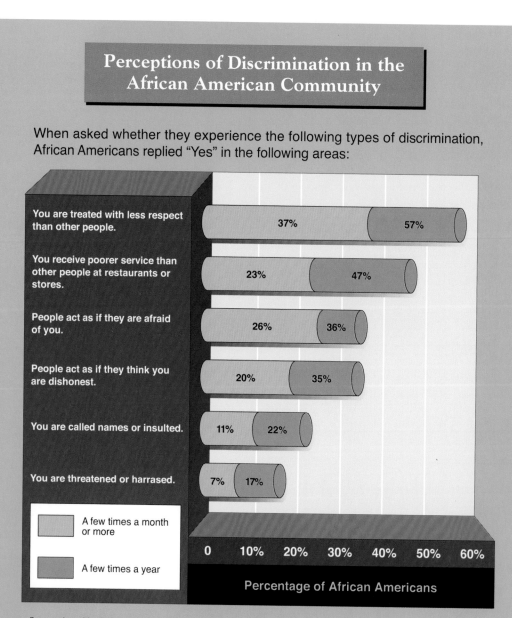

Perceptions of Discrimination in the African American Community

When asked whether they experience the following types of discrimination, African Americans replied "Yes" in the following areas:

- You are treated with less respect than other people. — 37% / 57%
- You receive poorer service than other people at restaurants or stores. — 23% / 47%
- People act as if they are afraid of you. — 26% / 36%
- People act as if they think you are dishonest. — 20% / 35%
- You are called names or insulted. — 11% / 22%
- You are threatened or harrased. — 7% / 17%

A few times a month or more

A few times a year

0   10%   20%   30%   40%   50%   60%

Percentage of African Americans

Source: Josephine Lovie, "We Don't Feel Welcome Here: African American and Hispanics in Metro Boston," Civil Rights Project, Harvard University, April 25, 2005.

The actions and words were undeniably clear. But our parents and other African-Americans worked diligently to steel us to take the onslaught and succeed despite it.

This Generation Has No Tools for Coping with Racism

Many millennials [kids who have come of age around 2000] have been spared both the brutality of racism at an early age as well as the black community's programming, deprogramming and reprogramming methods to help them cope.

Balogun, now a freshman at the University of Missouri–Kansas City, and her high school friend unfortunately got a harsh lesson served with what were supposed to be happy meals.

She told the panel that much work needs to be done to make King's dream of equality and opportunity for African-Americans a reality. She said progress has been made, "but we're going back in time."

"Our rights are slowly being taken away from us," Balogun said. "We are on the wrong path."

"We have to get out there and not only protest but work toward change."

Racism Has Not Gone Away

She said in an interview that it's not good that some people in their own country can't feel comfortable going out to eat with their friends just because they are African-American. "It was blatant racism," Balogun said.

Equally distressing was that her friend couldn't identify with what she had to endure. "It is a big, big, big, big problem," Balogun said.

I am glad she is aware of what she went through. Knowing that racism hasn't gone away is the first step needed toward vanquishing it once and for all.

TWO

Discrimination Against African Americans Is No Longer a Problem

Linda Chavez

In the following selection Linda Chavez argues that African Americans exaggerate the problem of discrimination. She complains that the leaders of the National Association for the Advancement of Colored People (NAACP) mistakenly see discrimination where it does not exist. Chavez states that discrimination is no longer a problem facing the black community; bigger obstacles include the high divorce rate among black families, lack of community leaders, and an increase in black-on-black crime. She suggests that if African Americans want to improve their educational, economic, and social standing in America, they need to stop blaming whites for their problems and look inside their communities for answers.

Chavez is chairman of the Center for Equal Opportunity. She writes a regular column for Townhall.com and is the author of *Betrayal: How Union Bosses Shake Down Their Members and Corrupt American Politics.*

The NAACP is America's oldest civil rights organization and for years stood as the moral conscience of the nation, fighting for the rights of black Americans to equal treatment at the polling booth, in the schoolhouse, in the courts and in the marketplace. How sad, now, that this venerable institution has been turned into a caricature of its former self.

The Irrelevance of the NAACP
Its leaders are stuck in a time warp, imagining they still live in a world of pick-ax- wielding bigots and lynch mobs. NAACP chairman Julian Bond, a veteran of the civil rights movement and a former Georgia state legislator, has been reduced to ugly name-calling in order to attract media attention. At the NAACP convention meeting in Florida, Bond accused the Republican Party of "appealing to the dark underside of American culture. . . . Their idea of

A teenage African American woman holds her child.

reparations is to give war criminal Jefferson Davis a pardon. Their idea of equal rights is the American flag and the Confederate swastika flying side by side," he told a cheering crowd.

The group no longer has an agenda, other than to "uproot the bigger '(B)ush' in 2004," as Bond promised. But the putatively nonpartisan group may run into problems fulfilling that goal, given its declining status.

Racism Is No Longer a Problem

The NAACP has become so irrelevant that even Democratic presidential aspirants—none of whom could hope to be elected without winning 90 percent of black votes nationwide—can afford to boycott the group's annual meeting. Senators Joe Lieberman and Dennis Kucinich and former Missouri congressman and House minority leader Dick Gephardt all had "other commitments" that prevented them from attending the convention.

Julian Bond may not recognize it, but racism is no longer the major problem facing American blacks. For the minority of black Americans—23 percent—who lived below the poverty line in 2001, discrimination isn't to blame.

What is? A list of likely culprits would surely include the collapse of the black family, the failure of the public schools and black-on-black crime.

Black Leaders Must Look Within the Community to Find Answers

National Center for Health statistics indicate that with two out of three black babies born to unwed mothers today, black children are far more likely to grow up poor than youngsters from any other group. And according to the Census Bureau, black children in single mother households are nearly five times more likely to live in poverty than are black children born to two-parent families; 47 percent of black youngsters under 18 who live in female-headed households are poor compared to only 10 percent who live with two parents. The problem of illegitimacy has plagued the black

Almost six in ten Americans say African American are treated with greater respect than in the past and many say the treatment of Hispanics has also improved.

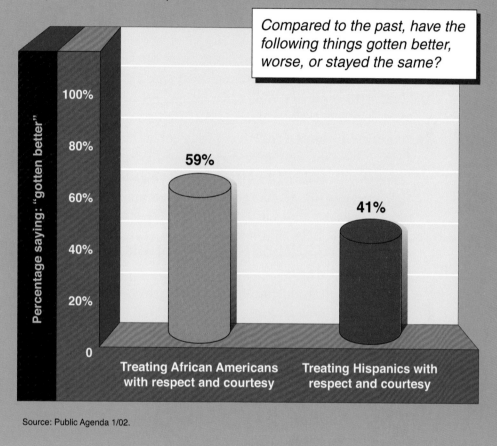

Compared to the past, have the following things gotten better, worse, or stayed the same?

Percentage saying: "gotten better"

59% — Treating African Americans with respect and courtesy

41% — Treating Hispanics with respect and courtesy

Source: Public Agenda 1/02.

community for nearly 40 years, but goes unaddressed by the NAACP or any other major black organization.

Julian Bond did talk about education in his convention address, but most of what he said took the form of vicious attacks on both Gov. Jeb Bush's and President Bush's education reform efforts. "Gov. Jeb Bush's notion of school reform is going to send black children to reform school," Bond said of Florida's efforts to put an end to promoting kids from grade to grade even if they haven't learned anything. So-called "social promotions" have resulted in schools graduating black high school seniors who—on average—read at the eighth-grade level.

Bond also talked about crime—but his sympathies were directed exclusively to the criminals. He bemoaned the sorry fact that 12 percent of all black men between the ages of 20 and 34 are incarcerated, and the NAACP has made voting rights for felons one of its top legislative priorities in recent years. But what about the black victims on whom these criminals prey, the men and women who work hard every day, only to be beaten, robbed, raped and murdered, not by Ku Klux Klansmen but by predators in their own communities? If the NAACP were truly concerned for the plight of black Americans, wouldn't it be pushing for more police and tougher sentences for violent offenders, not worrying about whether it can deliver more jailhouse votes to the Democratic Party?

African Americans Should Not Blame Others for Their Problems

There is much work left to be done if the lives of America's poorest blacks are to improve—but the NAACP seems to have little interest in tackling the really tough issues. Instead, its leaders would rather blame racism and Republicans and look to government to solve the problems of a community whose only hope is to heal itself.

THREE

Discrimination Against Arab Americans Is on the Rise

Kari Lydersen

> Since the terrorist attacks of September 11, 2001, Arab Americans have been increasingly discriminated against, argues author Kari Lydersen in the following selection. Lydersen charges that innocent Arabs and Arab Americans have been scapegoated, murdered, assaulted, and harassed. They have been the subjects of government campaigns to track their movements and have been detained without any evidence they are connected to a crime, according to Lydersen. Lydersen concludes that the current atmosphere is dangerous for Arab Americans, and is thus dangerous for anyone who cares about protecting the civil liberties and rights of all Americans.
>
> Lydersen is a journalist based in Chicago and an instructor for the Urban Youth International Journalism Program. Her articles have been published by *In These Times*, *Punk Planet*, *Clamor*, and *Impact Press*, from which this viewpoint was taken.

Just as the government is finally able to admit that it is wrong to arrest people for DWB [Driving While Black], it seems a new crime has been invented as part of the War on Terrorism. Call it EWA or just EWI. Existing While Arab, or more generally Existing While Immigrant.

Mourners pray at the casket of Arab American shopkeeper Abdo Ali Ahmed. He was murdered in a suspected hate crime not long after the September 11, 2001, terrorist attacks.

A License to Discriminate Against Arab Americans

With the war on terrorism giving President [George W.] Bush and [former] Attorney General [John] Ashcroft[1] carte blanche [white card, or license] to do almost anything they want, civil liberties and rights have been stripped away from the American public as a whole, and in particular, Arab-Americans and immigrants—even legal residents. As part of this campaign, the previously dirty words "racial profiling" are now considered legal policy and a valid strategy to fight terror. People can be searched, questioned, spied on, even detained without a lawyer on the basis of their race or religion alone. A Gallup poll taken shortly after the 9/11 attacks [the September 11, 2001, attacks on the World Trade Center and the

1. Ashcroft was replaced in 2005 by Attorney General Alberto Gonzales.

Pentagon] found that 60 percent of Americans supported racial profiling of Arabs at airports, and the Federal Motor Carrier Administration, which inspects trucks carrying hazardous materials, announced it would start searching Arab-looking drivers based on their race.

This despite the fact that experts on both the right and the left say that not only is racial profiling morally questionable, it is a completely inefficient and ineffective plan. They point out that the government is no more likely to catch a would-be terrorist by searching every Arab and immigrant than it is to find an armed robber by pulling over every Black driver.

"It's not just a bad thing, it's ineffective," said Ed Yohnka, director of communications for the ACLU [American Civil Liberties Union] of Illinois. "It's distracting from the real work that police ought to be doing. And it divides communities—the divisions created post-9/11 between Muslim and Southeast Asian communities and the police are very disturbing. It creates a kind of fear and anxiety in communities that doesn't serve any of us very well."

Generating Fear Through Scare Tactics

Yohnka is currently working on two cases involving profiling of African Americans, one in which three African-American high school students were searched and interrogated about drugs while driving to a game with their white coach, for no reason other than their race. He says the profiling of Arabs is no less onerous.

As with the war on drugs and crime, much of the public has been convinced to accept racial profiling through scare tactics.

"People are more willing to support the notion of profiling Arabs and Muslims than they were pre-9/11," said Yohnka. "They're more willing to support that than the profiling of African-Americans or Latinos. It's demonstrative of a certain kind of fear, a fear that the government often creates.". . .

"Unfair Treatment and Unkind Words"

Nine days after the September 11 attacks, President Bush said that, "No one should be singled out for unfair treatment or unkind words because of their ethnic background or religious faith." But his administration went full force into doing just this, and more, as did average citizens.

Racial profiling kicked in almost immediately after 9/11, first in the unofficial realm of discrimination, verbal insults and threats and hate crimes, then in official government policy. Average citizens carried out their own form of vigilante racial profiling in the wake of the attacks, with at least six Arab-Americans or Southeast Asians murdered around the country because of their ethnicity and countless hate-related assaults and acts of vandalism committed.

In Chicago alone, for example, 55 hate crimes were reported in which the attacks were mentioned and at least once an angry mob descended on a mosque. Mustapha Zemkour, a Chicago-area taxi driver, was beaten as his assailants yelled, "This is what you get, you mass murderer." The U.S. Justice Department's Civil Rights division has opened 403 federal investigations of anti-Arab hate crimes. Employment discrimination has also been common. The Equal Employment Opportunities Commission logged 671 complaints of anti-Arab related discrimination as of October 2002.

Holding Arab Americans Against Their Will

In November 2001, Ashcroft steam-rolled over public opinion and congressional opposition to institute a dragnet policy wherein 5,000 men of Arab descent were detained and questioned. This despite the fact he was advised against racial profiling by a panel of law enforcement specialists, as revealed in the internal memo "Assessing Behaviors" published in the *Boston Globe*.

Some of the men ended up being held for months with no evidence of wrongdoing before finally being released; others ended up being deported or detained indefinitely on minor visa violations. Many police departments around the country refused to participate in the dragnet, which did not end up yielding a single terrorism-related suspect and only about 20 visa violation charges. Nonetheless Ashcroft instituted a second dragnet of 3,000 nonimmigrant men.

A resolution passed six days after the attacks allows them to be held for 48 hours without charges, or longer in "emergency situations." Amnesty International has released a report detailing abuses and poor conditions these detainees have suffered, including solitary confinement and torture by guards in general population jails.

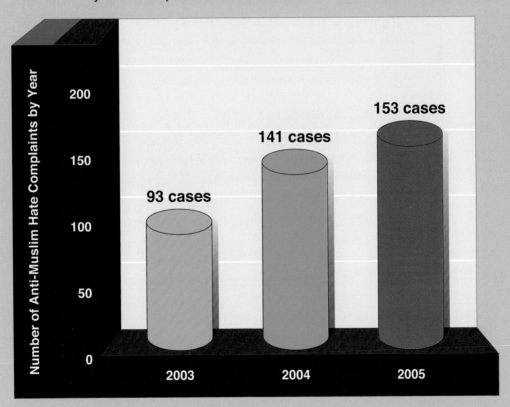

Anti-Muslim Hate Crime Complaints Are Increasing

Reports of hate crimes against Arabs and Muslims increases each year, according to the Council on American-Islamic Relations. In 2005 they rose 8.6 percent.

Source: Council on American-Islamic Relations, "The Status of Muslim Civil Rights in the United States, 2006," www.cair.org/pdf/2006-CAIR-Civil-Rights-Report.pdf.

"Sweeping and Blanket Accusations"

In June 2002, Ashcroft ordered the registration and fingerprinting of all legal visitors and immigrants from the Middle East and South Asia upon arrival in the U.S.

From December 2002 through February 2003, all men over age 16 from a list of Muslim countries and North Korea were required to register with the government, be fingerprinted and report any change in address, schooling or employment. Those who failed to register can be deported, even if they are legal residents, while many of those who did register were immediately arrested and interrogated for minor visa problems or just general "suspiciousness."

"Essentially the U.S. government has made sweeping and blanket accusations against people from foreign countries who the U.S. has foreign policy issues with," said Hatem Abudayyeh, a Palestinian activist and director of the Arab American Action Network in Chicago. "That's a blatant case of racial profiling."

In southern California, up to 1,000 men who reported for the December 16 registration deadline were detained, the majority of them Iranians, according to the National Immigration Forum. In L.A., up to one-fourth of those who reported for registration were put in deportation proceedings, even if they had been in the process of adjusting their immigration status. Abudayyeh noted that the focus on Iranians was especially illogical because rather than being supporters of the Iranian government, most long-time Iranian immigrants came here because they didn't support the government that took power in Iran after the 1979 Islamic revolution.

"These people have nothing to do with terrorism," said pro bono attorney Soheila Jonoubi. "They are all in the country legally. They have been singled out according to gender, ethnicity and religion. I have 16-year-old kids being pulled out of their mothers' arms crying and taken to jail."

"It Makes You Wonder"

The registrations took place with three different deadlines for different groups of countries. The first two groups included men from

Iraq, Iran, Libya, Yemen, Sudan and other countries. Saudi Arabia wasn't even included on the original list; now Saudis must register by a February 21 deadline.

"You don't even include people from the country where the majority of the hijackers came from," said Yohnka, before the later Saudi Arabia deadline was announced. "It makes you wonder how effective this thing could really be."

Abudayyeh sees both the original exclusion of U.S. ally Saudi Arabia from the list and the focus on Iranians as evidence of ulterior political motives. He thinks the focus on Iran, which Bush described as part of the "Axis of Evil," could be related to the …war with Iraq.

"Some people are saying that this was meant to be a clear message to Iranians here that if you even think about uniting with Iraq, you'll be attacked," he said. "Whether it's militarily attacked in the Gulf or through repression here." …

An Attack on All Communities of Color

People have also regularly been prohibited from flying at all because of their race. In June 2002, the Northern California ACLU and the law firm Relman & Associates filed a lawsuit against four airlines on behalf of the Arab Anti-Discrimination Committee and five men who were not allowed to fly because passengers or airline staff didn't like their appearance.

Racial profiling by citizens and the government in the war on terror has already had countless troubling outcomes, such as the arrest of three medical students on their way to school in Florida after a waitress reported they were planning a terrorist attack. A huge search effort yielded not a shred of evidence of any plan, and the government eventually apologized to the men, but they still were expelled from medical school for their supposed joking about September 11.

Incidents like this will only increase with the institution of things like the Terrorist Information and Prevention System (TIPS) program, which aimed to enlist employees like postal workers, deliverymen and meter readers in reporting on the personal lives and activities of their customers. The program was derailed thanks to outrage from the postal service, Congress and other agencies, but the general push to involve civilians in intelligence gathering continues.

"That's the Scary Part"

A report from the Illinois Coalition on Immigrant and Refugee Rights (ICIRR) notes that shortly after September 11, the FBI visited the home of Arab American Family Services co-director Itedal Shalabi on an anonymous tip that her son could be involved in terrorist activities. Her son is only nine years old.

"What would have happened if he was 16 or 17?" she asked. "That's the scary part."

FOUR

Discrimination Against Arab Americans Is Not on the Rise

Mary Ann Weston

The following selection is taken from a study on how Arab and Muslim Americans were portrayed in the news media following the September 11 terrorist attacks. The author, Mary Ann Weston, found that instead of stereotyping Arab and Muslim Americans, newspapers went to great lengths to portray them as kind, helpful, patriotic, and loyal citizens. She reports that the overwhelming majority of newspaper headlines and articles cast Arab and Muslim Americans as being innocent of wrongdoing and gave many a platform through which to humanize themselves in the eyes of the American public. Furthermore, writers, editors, and government officials rallied around the Arab and Muslim community, holding them up as exemplary of what it means to be American. Weston concludes that post–September 11 coverage of Arab and Muslim Americans did not discriminate but rather offered the public a sympathetic lens through which to view a vulnerable community. Weston is an associate professor in the Medill School of Journalism at Northwestern University.

A s newspapers across the country struggled to cover the cataclysms of Sept. 11, many focused on the local Arab American community. During the month following the attacks, several themes

Mary Ann Weston, "Post 9/11 Arab American Coverage Avoids Stereotypes," *Newspaper Research Journal*, vol. 24, Winter 2003, pp. 92-106. Copyright © 2003 Association for Education in Journalism and Mass Communication. Reproduced by permission.

evolved that were remarkably uniform in papers nationwide. In the days immediately after Sept. 11 stories concentrated on Arab Americans as double victims: They suffered as did everyone at the horror of the attacks; some lost loved ones. But at the same time they were being harassed, intimidated and discriminated against—even murdered—for events over which they had no control. The images these stories presented were overwhelmingly sympathetic ones of a people bewildered and victimized.

A Community Portrayed as Patriotic and Victimized

The *St. Louis Post-Dispatch* illustrated the innocence of local Arab Americans in a story knocking down a rumor that some Muslims cheered the attacks. "Muslim clerks at a 7-Eleven store in St. Louis reported that they were threatened Thursday in an incident that some in the Muslim and Arab-American community say highlights the danger of blaming many for the actions of a few terrorists." The story later quoted a clerk "who declined to be identified for fear of reprisals" this way: "'People think we have the religion, so we must be like (the terrorists),' said one employee, a 24-year-old Muslim born in Somalia who has lived in St. Louis for five years. 'My religion doesn't tell me to kill anybody. All those people who died were innocent.'"

Many stories highlighted Arab Americans' dual suffering in headlines, leads and quotes, as the following examples show.

Hartford Courant
"Arab Americans Deal with 'Dual Pain' after Attacks; While Mourning with Other Citizens, Some Feel Targeted for Their Ethnicity" (headline).

Detroit Free Press
"It was a sad, somber and tense day for Arab Americans across metro Detroit. They reacted with shock and outrage over Tuesday's terror attacks, as other Americans did. But they also feared they would again become victims of prejudice, of a racist sense they were not part of America." The story went on to quote an Arab American

leader as saying, "It's a double agony. . . . As U.S. citizens, we feel the tragedy, but we are also seen as being different, as suspects."

Cleveland Plain Dealer
"Local Arab-American leaders condemned yesterday's bombings as they braced for backlash, many expressing fears that their community would be blamed."

Sending the Message That Arab Americans Want to Help
Houston Chronicle
"Local Muslim and Arab leaders condemned the rash of terrorism Tuesday and pleaded with Americans not to mount a backlash based on race or religion."

Tampa Tribune
"Engineer Saleh Mubarak, a native of Syria, said Arab-Americans 'feel the pain twice,' once as Americans and again as targets of hostility and suspicion."

While highlighting their dual suffering, many stories also depicted Arab Americans as loyal and patriotic.

A *Washington Post* roundup on Sept. 13 [2001] noted that

> virtually every Muslim and Arab American group . . . Lined up yesterday to condemn the attacks on American targets. Leaders defended Islam as a peace-loving religion and insisted that their hearts and national loyalties were with America, not with foreign extremists.

A story in *Newsday* told of Arab and Sikh cab drivers who offered free rides to people searching for loved ones missing in the World Trade Center collapse.

> The cab drivers, fearing they are easy targets for harassment since the attack is being blamed on radical Middle Eastern Muslims, said they want to be embraced as American countrymen and not unjustly vilified as members of a murderous clan. They want to help.

The *Columbus Dispatch* profiled an Arab American, Mahmoud El-Yousseph, who was a 17-year member of the U.S. Air Force Reserve and Ohio Air National Guard and was awaiting call-up orders. Although his family had been threatened with firebombing, El-Yousseph was described as eager to go. "[The call-up] will give El-Yousseph a chance to show again that Arab-Americans are as loyal to this country as anyone," the story said. "'It will be a bit of a hardship on my family, but my bags are packed and I'm ready to go; I'd be proud to go,'" he said yesterday.

And the *Detroit Free Press* quoted a local Arab American fearful of hate crimes as saying, "We're Americans just like everyone else, and we're hurt by the attack. . . . I was born in Cleveland. You can't get more American than that."

In these and many other examples Arab Americans and Muslims were portrayed sympathetically. By directly quoting local individuals, the stories humanized Arab Americans, portraying them as part of the community. Thus Arab Americans' own words were implicit refutations of the evil, menacing terrorist image.

The theme of Arab Americans as fearful of a backlash was revisited after the U.S. bombing of Afghanistan began in early October. Such stories depicted Arab Americans as publicly supportive of the bombings, but fearful of civilian casualties and domestic backlash.

The Country Rallied Around Arab and Muslim Americans

Another theme that emerged after the initial wave of stories about hate crimes against Arab Americans was the outpouring of sympathy and support for them. Such stories surged after President George W. Bush visited a mosque on Sept. 17. For example a *Chicago Tribune* story said,

> Across the city and suburbs . . . some people called mosques to offer emotional and financial support, walking Muslim children to school and leaving in the parking lot of the Islamic Association of Des Plaines an anonymous gift of yellow flowers with the note: "May all your families be safe."

A *USA Today* story profiled an Arab American family in Aurora, Colo., who had been harassed and intimidated. Women in the family, wearing hijab, were afraid to go out. The story related how a Jewish couple from across the street, "previously known only by looks and nods," came to the door. They invited the Arab Americans for honey cake and coffee to celebrate Rosh Hashanah, the Jewish

A peace and healing rally in Atlanta on September 21, 2001. Many Americans of different backgrounds reacted to the September 11 attacks by voicing support for Arab and Muslim American communities and calling for tolerance.

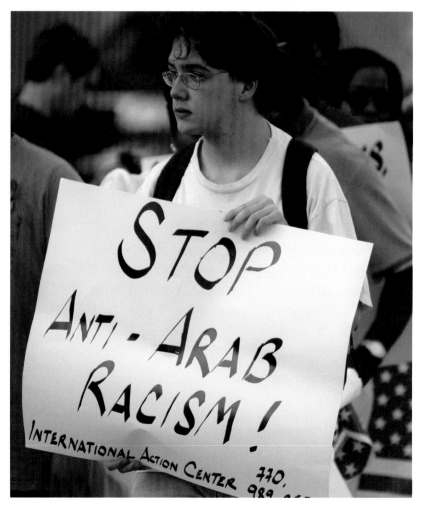

New Year. "We just want you to know that we feel for you right now," said the neighbor.

A *Plain Dealer* story described a woman who

> rallied several friends and drove up [to Cleveland] from Mansfield, determined to patronize Arab merchants after learning they felt threatened. "This is not the response that we need to have to this terrible tragedy," [the woman] said. "I can't do much, but give blood—which I did yesterday—and go shopping."

Stories of individual families' pain and of the kindness of strangers depicted Arab Americans sympathetically as innocent victims embraced by the larger community.

In All Communities, Support Was Offered

Numerous stories showed local leaders—governors and mayors—making statements of support and warning of the criminal consequences of ethnic intimidation. Some stories drew contrasts between this official support and the way the Arab American community had been shunned by candidates previously. "[T]hey have emerged from one of the most maligned, politically powerless immigrant groups in American history into a viable political lobby," a *Chicago Tribune* article noted. It observed that Arab American votes were actively courted by both candidates in the 2000 presidential election, in contrast to rejections of Arab Americans by Democratic Presidential candidates Walter Mondale in 1984 and Michael Dukakis in 1988 and by New York Senate candidate Hillary Rodham Clinton in 2000.

Using the Past to Improve the Future

Still other stories drew parallels between the travails of Arab Americans and the internment of Japanese Americans after Pearl Harbor. A *Chicago Tribune* story began,

> Amid reports of hate crimes, assaults and even killings of innocent people with Arab names, Japanese-Americans are tak-

ing the lead in efforts to support Arab-Americans even as they recall World War II, when their fellow Americans vilified them for Japan's actions.

This association with Japanese Americans, whose treatment has been discredited and whose loyalty is undeniable, contributed to the positive and patriotic image of Arab Americans.

A more ambiguous image of Arab Americans emerged from stories about the government's search for the roots of the terrorism plot. Arab Americans were caught astride the shifting line between civil liberties and national security. Some stories described their uneasy relationship with the government, which they praised for prosecuting hate crimes and feared for its dragnet of Middle Eastern men. A *Los Angeles Times* story reflected these complexities when it reported Muslim leaders suggested that a surge in hate crimes was fueled by the FBI's detention of "dozens of people of Middle Eastern heritage for questioning in its terrorist investigation, most of them on immigration charges unconnected to last week's hijackings." By juxtaposing President Bush's call for religious tolerance, the surge of hate crimes and Muslim complaints about the FBI's roundup of Middle Eastern men, the story legitimized the Muslims' concerns.

In another example, an *Atlanta Journal and Constitution* story said,

Arab-Americans feel that the [Bush] administration they hoped would redress their grievances has instituted policies that disproportionately target them, including indefinitely detaining people of Middle Eastern descent on suspicion of terrorism.

An Effort to Show Arab Americans Fairly

By prominently showcasing Arab Americans' concerns, such stories contributed to an image of Arab Americans as solid citizens with grievances and helped diminish their image as outsiders, law breakers or worse. Other stories implicitly challenged the FBI roundup by highlighting Arab Americans' complaints about being taken off airplanes and having worship services disrupted.

"[Arab Americans] believe that they are being singled out by federal agents and airlines for suspicion, hostility and unfair treatment simply because of their ethnic background and religion," a *Pittsburgh Post-Gazette* story said.

Finally, a few stories quoted Arab Americans who sought to explain possible motivations for the attacks, while emphatically not condoning them. However much such ideas may have been discussed within the community, apparently few wished to express them on the record. In the stories analyzed, those making the explanations were not named. The dilemma of those who sought to explain the terrorists' actions was clearly and sympathetically put in a (New Orleans) *Times-Picayune* story quoting an unnamed spokeswoman for an Arab American group. "[L]ike so many Arab-Americans, the spokeswoman said she fears explanations will be mistaken for excuses. For this reason, she has asked not to be identified."

Post-9/11 Treatment of Arab Americans Was Not Discriminatory

Before Sept. 11 Arab Americans were not prominently in the news. Their media image, conflated with that of Arabs and Muslims abroad, was negative. Thus, when Arab Americans became suddenly newsworthy, their portrayals in newspapers had considerable resonance. What did the stories tell readers about Arab and Muslim cultures, religions and origins? . . .

A dominant theme of pre–Sept. 11 stories was of Arab Americans resisting stereotypes and discrimination. In the month after Sept. 11 Arab Americans surged onto the news agenda. Newspaper readers saw them depicted sympathetically as doubly victimized, as loyal, patriotic members of the community, as targets of government detentions. The images often contained intimate views of nearby individuals and sometimes revealing descriptions of their cultures and religion. Though stories examined often failed to depict the diversity of Arab American culture, few grossly inaccurate or offensive portrayals were found. Such portrayals contrast vividly with the historic stereotype of the Arab terrorist. Future research may discern whether the diverse and positive images of 2001 have established a competing narrative to the heretofore-dominant negative stereotypes.

FIVE

Discrimination Against Latinos Is Increasing

Andrew Stephen

In the following selection author Andrew Stephen documents an increasing mood of discrimination and racism
aimed at Latinos in the United States. Stephen argues that
many Americans treat Latinos as financial and social bur-
dens when in reality they are hard-working, patriotic citizens and residents. Even in past eras, Latino citizens such
as Mexican Americans have been repeatedly mistreated,
even kicked out of the country during times of political
upheaval. Stephen points out that as the Latino population
grows, those most resistant to their presence will be forced
to change their attitude as they realize they need Latino
votes to win elections. Stephen concludes that discrimination against Latino Americans and immigrants is unfair and
must be brought to a swift halt.

Stephen is the U.S. editor of the *New Statesman*, from
which this viewpoint was taken. He is also a regular con-
tributor to BBC news programs and to the *New York Times*
and *Sunday Times Magazine*.

I first visited the United States as a teenager in 1970, when the
number of people living here who had been born abroad was 9.6
million. Just a decade later, it had risen to 14.1 million. By 1990 the

Andrew Stephen, "The Latino Giant Awakes," *New Statesman* (1996), vol. 135, May 1, 2006, pp.
30-31. Copyright © 2006 *New Statesman*, Ltd. Reproduced by permission.

figure was 19.1 million, and in 2000 there were 31.1 million people living in the US who had not actually been born here. Overall, according to the Centre for Immigration Studies, 7.9 million people have moved to the US in the past five years—two and a half times the total that came in the last record wave of European immigration, a century ago.

An Anti-immigrant Atmosphere

But if you think this means America is still a land that welcomes the tired, poor and huddled masses yearning to breathe free—to quote those wonderfully idealistic words by Emma Lazarus, written in 1883 and still proudly exhibited on the Statue of Liberty as if they were true—think again. Isn't this, after all, a nation of immigrants that constantly strengthens itself with new blood and brains? The likes of Bill Gates and Microsoft certainly want it to be: not long ago he made a rare visit to Washington to lobby for more visas to be granted to people from countries such as India, because he knows from personal experience that well-educated youngsters from these backgrounds have the know-how and eagerness that native-born Americans simply do not possess.

Nor is there any good reason why America cannot take a limitless number of such immigrants for the foreseeable future: it is a land so huge that there are still only 30 people on average living in each square kilometre, compared with 243 for (say) Britain. European immigrants were welcomed with food, medicine, beds, showers and documentation on Ellis Island a century ago; but any day now my friend [former Republican Senator] Bill Frist, . . . will introduce a bill to order fleets of helicopters and surveillance aircraft, the construction of giant concrete walls, and $2 billion-worth of "border-patrol agents" to keep immigrants out of the land of the free.

"An Ugly Mood of Racism"

Frist is basically a decent fellow too. Yet there is an ugly mood of racism sweeping this country in which the casually brutal word "illegal" is used as a noun, even by the most enlightened, to describe fellow human beings who live and work here but do not have the documentation to do so legally (though that in itself is only a felony, rather than a crime). Every weekday evening at six o'clock on CNN, there is a "news" programme, fronted by a foaming, red-faced fellow called Lou Dobbs, and dominated by racist, anti-immigrant diatribes that are positively fascistic (and I do not use the word lightly). In such a climate, the "Minutemen"—the white, self-appointed

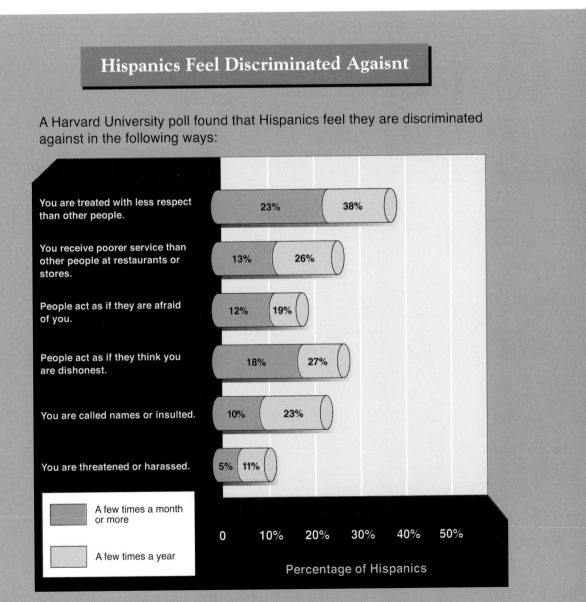

Hispanics Feel Discriminated Agaisnt

A Harvard University poll found that Hispanics feel they are discriminated against in the following ways:

You are treated with less respect than other people.
23% 38%

You receive poorer service than other people at restaurants or stores.
13% 26%

People act as if they are afraid of you.
12% 19%

People act as if they think you are dishonest.
18% 27%

You are called names or insulted.
10% 23%

You are threatened or harassed.
5% 11%

A few times a month or more

A few times a year

0   10%   20%   30%   40%   50%

Percentage of Hispanics

Source: Josephine Lovie, "We Don't Feel Welcome Here: African American and Hispanics in Metro Boston," Civil Rights Project, Harvard University, April 25, 2005.

"vigilantes" who venture into border deserts at night armed with shotguns to hunt down illegals—are the patriotic heroes of our times.

The difference between this anger of 2006 and the complacently white-dominated America of Walter Cronkite and Lucille Ball to which I came as a teenager is simple: in 1970, 63 per cent of the immigrants to the US had been born in Europe or Canada, but today the newcomers are mostly Latino. To put it simply, most Americans do not want brown wogs—and especially not when, relying on figures from reputable bodies such as the Pew Hispanic Centre, between 11 million and 12 million of them can be contemptuously dismissed as illegals. I repeatedly come across white Americans dismayed that their country has so rapidly become one-seventh Hispanic. Nothing enrages them more than when they hear the computerised voice that answers the phone, "For English, press 1 . . . for Spanish, press 2," followed by the same announcement in Spanish.

America Discriminates Against Latinos—but Needs Them Too

All this puts Bill Frist, George W. Bush et al in a quandary, however. They know that most white Republican voters, worked into a frenzy by the likes of Lou, want a bill that is much more swingeing than the one Frist is proposing, but they also realise that—to paraphrase Fernand Braudel—capitalism knows no boundaries, and that American business craves not only legal computer whizzes from India but also illegal cheap labour.

Illegal workers, after all, are needed to do jobs that Americans spurn: house-cleaning, fruit-picking and looking after rich white brats. To take just one specific example: the American Farm Bureau, perhaps the lead lobbying group for US agriculture, says that the US would lose between $5 billion and $9 billion a year in fruit, vegetable and flower production if "guest workers" (the language becomes quaintly benign when the speaker seeks a different emphasis) were not able to sweat in the fields for a pittance.

This, the imperative of Braudellian economics, is problem one for the Republicans. Problem two is purely political: even though

Kevin and Estrella Gonzalez participate in a rally outside the federal court in Scranton, Pennsylvania. They are calling for the court to strike down local laws in nearby Hazelton that punish businesses for employing illegal immigrants.

a significant proportion of these newcomers do not have the vote because they are illegals, the Hispanic vote is of crucial importance to all politicians, Republican or Democrat. No candidate making a speech in recent presidential campaigns has failed to throw in a few words of Spanish at the first chance, so he can appear on the Spanish-language TV stations that evening. "!Si, se puede!" ("Yes, we can!") thundered the triumphant chant of Hispanics as they marched through DC on 10 April. "The sleeping Latino giant is finally awake," said Jaime Contreras, president of the National Capital Immigrant Coalition.

The Irony of Discrimination Toward Latinos

Previous big-time Republicans underestimated the sleeping giant to their cost. A former senator named Pete Wilson ran his 1994 campaign for the governorship of California on a platform of denying benefits, education and healthcare to illegals ("they just keep coming"). He proceeded to win the seat by a landslide and was even thought, briefly, to be a contender for the presidency. But then Hispanic political groups got their act together, his governorship fell into disarray and he was run out of office, never to be heard from again (certainly not by me).

I find terrible ironies about the wave of racism being directed towards America's Latinos, 78 per cent of whom are Mexican. For example, in all the millions of words written or spoken on the subject in the US media in recent weeks, I have not come across a single reference to the fact that large chunks of the US where their presence is seen as so problematic—Texas, New Mexico, California itself—were part of Mexico until they were forcibly seized by the US in 1846–48, in what is still proudly referred to in the school textbooks here as American "expansionism", carried out in the name of the nation's self-proclaimed Manifest Destiny. The rest of Mexico was invaded by the US army then, too, and escaped the same fate only when congressmen realised that the result of seizing the entire territory would be millions of brown US citizens—something said openly then, but only covertly now.

Nor have I ever seen one single textbook that mentions how Mexican Americans—including legal residents and even US citizens—were kicked out and sent to Mexico during the Great Depression. It's true, though, American readers: check it out. The final irony is that the Latino newcomers are a remarkably peaceful, hard-working and gentle lot: one academic study found that Hispanic immigrants are 45 per cent less likely to commit violence than third-generation Americans.

Discrimination Against Latinos Must End

Nevertheless, polls by both *Time* and the Pew Research Centre find that Americans believe—by majorities of 68 and 74 per cent, respectively—that (in the words of one question in the Pew poll) "immigrants today are a burden on our country because they take our jobs, housing and healthcare". There are some respected academics, such as Professor George Borjas of Harvard, who argue that the arrival of immigrants has lowered the incomes of established Americans by as much as 5 per cent; the general consensus, however, is that their presence has had the effect of raising it very slightly, perhaps by less than 1 per cent.

What is indubitable is that the lives of many white Americans would fall apart without the work of Latinos. I know of one lady in San Dimas in California, for example, who was aghast when her gardener (an illegal immigrant, naturally) told her the climate of fear was such that he could no longer risk driving to work without a driving licence. So she did what any self-respecting wealthy white woman in California would do: she promptly hired him a chauffeur of his own. Without Hispanics, after all, who would trim our hedges, cut our grass and unblock our sewage pipes?

SIX

Women Are Discriminated Against in the Workplace

Martha Burk

> Women continue to be paid less than men, argues author Martha Burk in the following selection. Burk reports that on average women make 76 cents to a man's dollar for comparable positions, duties, and shifts. She discusses a bill known as the Fair Pay Act that would help bridge this divide in salary, lamenting that it has been repeatedly rejected by various politicians and judges. Burk challenges companies to make public the wages they pay their male and female employees so workers can decide for themselves if they want to work for a company that rewards employees for their gender rather than their performance.
>
> Burk is the money editor for *Ms. Magazine* and author of *Cult of Power: Sex Discrimination in the Workplace and What Can Be Done About It.*

We're coming up on Equal Pay Day again. That's the day in April every year—this year the 24th—when women's earnings finally catch up with what men made by Dec. 31 of the previous year. Women's groups, led by the National Committee on Pay Equity, will rally on Capitol Hill to call attention to the issue.

Women Continue to Be Paid Less than Men

The pay gap is still a stubborn problem, with women who work full time year-round making 76 cents to a man's dollar. Though it consistently polls No. 1 with female voters in election years, politicians don't seem motivated to do much about it.

Some people say pay disparities between women and men are an illusion—women just like to choose jobs that pay less because they're not as risky or have shorter hours. But the data don't

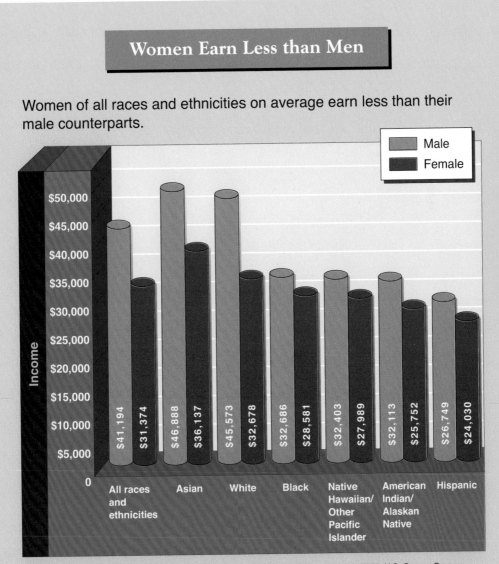

Women Earn Less than Men

Women of all races and ethnicities on average earn less than their male counterparts.

Male
Female

Income

$50,000
$45,000
$40,000
$35,000
$30,000
$25,000
$20,000
$15,000
$10,000
$5,000
0

All races and ethnicities: $41,194 / $31,374
Asian: $46,888 / $36,137
White: $45,573 / $32,678
Black: $32,686 / $28,581
Native Hawaiian/Other Pacific Islander: $32,403 / $27,989
American Indian/Alaskan Native: $32,113 / $25,752
Hispanic: $26,749 / $24,030

Source: "Income, Earnings and Poverty from the American Community Survey," August 2005, U.S. Census Bureau.

back up these claims. Even when researchers take into account such factors as part-time work or time out of the work force to care for kids, the numbers show that men make more. Another problem that just won't go away is that so-called "men's jobs," like plumbing, pay more than "women's jobs," like nursing. That tells us something about what we value as a society, and it's not women's work.

The Fair Pay Act, a bill that would help narrow the gap, has grown old bouncing around Capitol Hill since the early 1990s,

These are four of the original plaintiffs in a major class-action lawsuit claiming that Wal-Mart discriminated against its female employees.

never receiving as much as a hearing. If the FPA ever passed, it would require employers to rate their jobs on skill, effort, responsibility and working conditions, and equalize pay for comparable jobs even if the job titles and duties are different. Employers naturally resist this, citing loss of "competitive advantage," but women's advocates suspect the real reason is that the numbers would be too damning. Women might even get big ideas like suing their employers for sex discrimination in pay and promotion, as female workers at Wal-Mart have done in the largest class-action suit in history.

Discriminated Against in Salary and Attitude

A new book released this month from The Feminist Press—*Taking on the Big Boys* by Ellen Bravo, longtime CEO of 9 to 5, an advocacy organization for working women—attacks the pay equity issue head on. Bravo enlightens the reader in a no-nonsense way on deep-seated workplace attitudes and practices that hinder women's progress on the pay front. More importantly, she shows us how public policy is influenced through a variety of tactics used by opponents. One such tactic is catastrophizing, meaning predicting the downfall of capitalism as we know it if women catch up with men in earnings. Poster boy for this tactic is Chief Justice John Roberts, who dismissed the concept in the FPA as a "pernicious" redistribution of wealth, saying, "Their slogan may as well be 'From each according to his ability, to each according to her gender.'" Pretty scary stuff for the women of Wal-Mart, should their case, now on appeal, reach the Supremes.

Taking on the Big Boys shows us how continued monitoring and enforcement will be necessary, even for companies that want to do better. The FPA also contains a provision that would require companies to report earnings by race and gender in each job category—not anybody's salary on a bulletin board, but just overall statistics, so women could see how they were faring compared to the guys in the company overall.

Companies Should Disclose Salary Information

While there's no law now that says companies have to disclose how they pay and promote their workers, there's no law that says they can't. Wal-Mart agreed last year under stockholder pressure to post its EEO-1 form online, showing broad job categories by race and gender (the form does not include pay data). Some disclosure is better than none, but all companies should go a step further and release pay data for women and men by job category, as Ben & Jerry's has done for years. If pay scales are equitable, there should be nothing to hide. Women could see right up front if the company is fair. It would eliminate the need for lawsuits and create tremendous employee loyalty and customer good will. That ought to be worth 24 extra cents in the pay envelope.

Racial Profiling Is Discriminatory

U.S. Department of Justice

The following selection is taken from the U.S. Department of Justice's guidelines for law enforcement. It rejects racial profiling on the grounds that it is discriminatory, in violation of the Constitution, and results in poor police work. When suspects are investigated because of their race or ethnicity, officers tend to reach sloppy and erroneous conclusions, oftentimes while the real perpetrator gets away. In addition, the authors argue that racial profiling makes the American public distrust police officers and other law enforcement agents, making their jobs even more difficult. The Department of Justice outlines certain circumstances in which it is acceptable to factor race into a law enforcement incident—for example, if officers were to apprehend a suspect based on a specific identifying quality noticed at the scene of a crime. But on the whole, the Department of Justice concludes that all of its officers are prohibited from using racial profiling on the grounds that it is a discriminatory and ineffective practice.

U.S. Department of Justice, "Racial Profiling Fact Sheet," June, 2003.

"It's wrong, and we will end it in America. In so doing, we will not hinder the work of our nation's brave police officers. They protect us every day—often at great risk. But by stopping the abuses of a few, we will add to the public confidence our police officers earn and deserve."

—President George W. Bush, Feb. 27, 2001

"This administration . . . has been opposed to racial profiling and has done more to indicate its opposition than ever in history. The President said it's wrong and we'll end it in America, and I subscribe to that. Using race . . . as a proxy for potential criminal behavior is unconstitutional, and it undermines law enforcement by undermining the confidence that people can have in law enforcement."

—Attorney General John Ashcroft, Feb. 28, 2002

Racial Profiling Is Wrong and Will Not Be Tolerated

Racial profiling sends the dehumanizing message to our citizens that they are judged by the color of their skin and harms the criminal justice system by eviscerating the trust that is necessary if law enforcement is to effectively protect our communities.

- **America has a moral obligation to prohibit racial profiling.** Race-based assumptions in law enforcement perpetuate negative racial stereotypes that are harmful to our diverse democracy, and materially impair our efforts to maintain a fair and just society. As Attorney General John Ashcroft[1] said, racial profiling creates a "lose-lose" situation because it destroys the potential for underlying trust that "should support the administration of justice as a societal objective, not just as a law enforcement objective."

- **The overwhelming majority of federal law enforcement officers perform their jobs with dedication, fairness and honor, but any instance of racial profiling by a few damages our criminal justice system.** The vast majority of federal law enforce-

1. Ashcroft was replaced in 2005 by Attorney General Alberto Gonzales.

ment officers are hard-working public servants who perform a dangerous job with dedication, fairness and honor. However, when law enforcement practices are perceived to be biased or unfair, the general public, and especially minority communities, are less willing to trust and confide in officers, report crimes, be witnesses at trials, or serve on juries.

- **Racial profiling is discrimination, and it taints the entire criminal justice system.** Racial profiling rests on the erroneous assumption that any particular individual of one race or ethnicity is more likely to engage in misconduct than any particular individual of other races or ethnicities.

Taking Steps to Ban Racial Profiling
Due to the seriousness of racial profiling, the Justice Department has developed guidelines to make clear that it is prohibited in federal law enforcement.

- **President Bush has directed that racial profiling be formally banned.** In his February 27, 2001, Address to a Joint Session of Congress, President George W. Bush declared that racial profiling is "wrong and we will end it in America." He directed the Attorney General to review the use by federal law enforcement authorities of race as a factor in conducting stops, searches and other law enforcement investigative procedures. The Attorney General, in turn, instructed the Civil Rights Division to develop guidance for federal officials to ensure an end to racial profiling in federal law enforcement.

- **The Bush administration is the first to take action to ban racial profiling in federal law enforcement.** The guidance has been sent to all federal law enforcement agencies and is effective immediately. Federal agencies will review their policies and procedures to ensure compliance.

- **The guidance requires more restrictions on the use of race by federal law enforcement than does the Constitution.** The

As part of an effort to identify and stop racial profiling by Rhode Island police, state attorney general Sheldon Whitehouse unveils a new form that all police will be required to fill out after every traffic stop.

guidance in many cases imposes *more* restrictions on the use of race and ethnicity in federal law enforcement than the Constitution requires. This guidance prohibits racial profiling in federal law enforcement practices without hindering the important work of our nation's public safety officials, particularly the intensified anti-terrorism efforts precipitated by the attacks of September 11, 2001.

- **Prohibiting racial profiling in routine or spontaneous activities in domestic law enforcement:** In making routine or spontaneous law enforcement decisions, such as ordinary traffic stops, federal law enforcement officers may *not* use race or ethnicity to any degree, except that officers may rely on race and ethnicity if a specific suspect description exists. This prohibition applies even where the use of race or ethnicity might otherwise be lawful.

Stereotyping Has No Place in Good Police Work

- **Routine patrol duties must be carried out without consideration of race**. Federal law enforcement agencies and officers sometimes engage in law enforcement activities, such as traffic and foot patrols, that generally do not involve either the ongoing investigation of specific criminal activities or the prevention of catastrophic events or harm to the national security. Rather, their activities are typified by spontaneous action in response to the activities of individuals whom they happen to encounter in the course of their patrols and about whom they have no information other than their observations. These general enforcement responsibilities should be carried out without *any* consideration of race or ethnicity.

  - *Example*: While parked by the side of the highway, a federal officer notices that nearly all vehicles on the road are exceeding the posted speed limit. Although each such vehicle is committing an infraction that would legally justify a stop, the officer may not use race or ethnicity as a factor in deciding which motorists to pull over. Likewise, the officer may not use race or ethnicity in deciding which detained motorists to ask to consent to a search of their vehicles.

- **Stereotyping certain races as having a greater propensity to commit crimes is absolutely prohibited**. Some have argued that overall discrepancies in crime rates among racial groups could justify using race as a factor in general traffic enforcement activities and would produce a greater number of arrests for non-traffic offenses (*e.g.*, narcotics trafficking). We emphatically reject this view. It is patently unacceptable and thus prohibited under this guidance for federal law enforcement officers to engage in racial profiling.

- **Acting on specific suspect identification does not constitute impermissible stereotyping.** The situation is different when a federal officer acts on the personal identifying characteristics of potential suspects, including age, sex, ethnicity or race. Common sense dictates that when a victim or witness describes the assailant as being of a particular race, authorities may properly limit their search for suspects to persons of that race. In such circumstances, the federal officer is not acting based on a generalized assumption about persons of different races; rather, the officer is helping locate a specific individual previously identified as involved in [a] crime.

  - *Example:* While parked by the side of the highway, a federal officer receives an "All Points Bulletin" to be on the look-out for a fleeing bank robbery suspect, a man of a particular race and particular hair color in his 30s driving a blue automobile. The officer may use this description, including the race of the particular suspect, in deciding which speeding motorists to pull over.

- **Prohibiting racial profiling in federal law enforcement activities related to specific investigations**: In conducting activities in connection with a specific investigation, federal law enforcement officers may consider race and ethnicity only to the extent that there is trustworthy information, relevant to the locality or time frame, that links persons of a particular race or ethnicity to an identified criminal incident, scheme, or organization. This standard applies even where the use of race or ethnicity might otherwise be lawful.

- **Acting on specific information does not constitute impermissible stereotyping.** Often federal officers have specific information, based on trustworthy sources, to "be on the lookout" for specific individuals identified at least in part by race or ethnicity. In such circumstances, the officer is not acting based on a generalized assumption about persons of different races; rather, the officer is helping locate specific individuals previously identified as involved in [a] crime.

- *Example:* In connection with a new initiative to increase drug arrests, federal authorities begin aggressively enforcing speeding, traffic, and other public area laws in a neighborhood predominantly occupied by people of a single race. The choice of neighborhood was not based on the number of 911 calls,

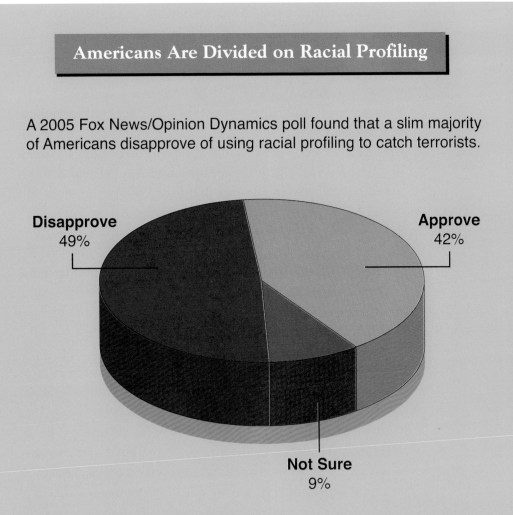

Americans Are Divided on Racial Profiling

A 2005 Fox News/Opinion Dynamics poll found that a slim majority of Americans disapprove of using racial profiling to catch terrorists.

Disapprove
49%

Approve
42%

Not Sure
9%

Source: Fox News/Opinion Dynamics Poll, July 29, 2005.

number of arrests, or other pertinent reporting data specific to that area, but only on the general assumption that more drug-related crime occurs in that neighborhood because of its racial composition. This effort would be *improper* because it is based on generalized stereotypes.

- *Example*: The victim of an assault at a local university describes her assailant as a young male of a particular race with a cut on his right hand. The investigation focuses on whether any students at the university fit the victim's description. Here investigators are properly relying on a description given by the victim, part of which included the assailant's race. Although the ensuing investigation affects students of a particular race, that investigation is not undertaken with a discriminatory purpose. Thus use of race as a factor in the investigation, in this instance, is permissible.

- **Reliance upon generalized stereotypes continues to be absolutely forbidden.** Use of race or ethnicity is permitted only when the federal officer is pursuing a specific lead concerning the identifying characteristics of persons involved in an *identified* criminal activity. The rationale underlying this concept carefully limits its reach. In order to qualify as a legitimate investigative lead, the following must be true:

  - The information must be relevant to the locality or time frame of the criminal activity;

  - The information must be trustworthy; and,

  - The information concerning identifying characteristics must be tied to a particular criminal incident, a particular criminal scheme, or a particular criminal organization.

  - *Example*: The FBI is investigating the murder of a known gang member and has information that the shooter is a member of a rival gang. The FBI knows that the members of the rival gang are exclusively members of a certain ethnicity. This information, however, is not suspect-specific because there is no description of the particular assailant. But because authorities have reliable, locally relevant information linking a rival group with a distinctive ethnic character to the murder, federal law enforcement officers could properly consider ethnicity in conjunction with other appropriate factors in the course of conducting their investigation. Agents could properly decide to focus on persons dressed in a manner consistent with gang activity, but ignore persons dressed in that manner who do not appear to be members of that particular ethnicity.

- *Example*: While investigating a car theft ring that dismantles cars and ships the parts for sale in other states, the FBI is informed by local authorities that it is common knowledge locally that most car thefts in that area are committed by individuals of a particular race. In this example, although the source (local police) is trustworthy, and the information potentially verifiable with reference to arrest statistics, there is no particular incident- or scheme-specific information linking individuals of that race to the particular interstate ring the FBI is investigating. Thus, agents could not use ethnicity as a factor in making law enforcement decisions in this investigation.

Taking Steps to Balance National Security Concerns

The Justice Department's policy guidance ensures that federal law enforcement continues to have the tools needed to identify terrorist threats and stop potential catastrophic attacks.

- **Federal law enforcement will continue terrorist identification.** Since the terrorist attacks on September 11, 2001, the President has emphasized that federal law enforcement personnel must use every legitimate tool to prevent future attacks, protect our nation's borders, and deter those who would cause devastating harm to our country and its people through the use of biological or chemical weapons, other weapons of mass destruction, suicide hijackings, or any other means.

- Therefore, the racial profiling guidance recognizes that race and ethnicity may be used in terrorist identification, but only to the extent permitted by the nation's laws and the Constitution. The policy guidance emphasizes that, even in the national security context, the constitutional restriction on use of generalized stereotypes remains.

- **Federal law enforcement must adhere to limitations imposed by the Constitution.** In investigating or preventing threats to national security or other catastrophic events (including the performance of duties related to air transportation security), or in enforcing laws protecting the integrity of the nation's borders, federal law enforcement officers may not consider race or ethnicity except to the extent permitted by the Constitution and laws of the United States.

  - **The Constitution prohibits consideration of race or ethnicity in law enforcement decisions in all but the most exceptional instances.** Given the incalculably high stakes involved in such investigations, federal law enforcement officers who are protecting national security or preventing catastrophic events (as well as airport security screeners) may consider race, ethnicity, alienage, and other relevant factors. Constitutional provisions limiting government action on the basis of race are wide-ranging and provide substantial protections at every step of the investigative and judicial process. Accordingly, this policy will honor the rule of law and promote vigorous protection of our national security.

  - **Federal law enforcement must guard against uncertain threats of terrorism.** Because terrorist organizations might aim to engage in unexpected acts of catastrophic violence in any available part of the country (indeed, in multiple places simultaneously, if possible), there can be no expectation that the information must be specific to a particular locale or even to a particular identified scheme.

- **Even in the national security context, reliance upon generalized stereotypes is restricted by the Constitution**. For example, at the security entrance to a federal courthouse, a man who appears to be of a particular ethnicity properly submits his briefcase for x-ray screening and passes through the metal detector. The inspection of the briefcase reveals nothing amiss. The man does not activate the metal detector, and there is nothing suspicious about his activities or appearance. Absent any threat warning or other particular reason to suspect that those of the man's apparent ethnicity pose a heightened danger to the courthouse, the federal security screener may not order the man to undergo a further inspection solely because of his apparent ethnicity.

  - *Example*: U.S. intelligence sources report that Middle Eastern terrorists are planning to use commercial jetliners as weapons by hijacking them at an airport in California during the next week. Before allowing men appearing to be of Middle Eastern origin to board commercial airplanes in California airports during the next week, Transportation Security Administration personnel, and other federal and state authorities, may subject them to heightened scrutiny.

  - *Example*: The FBI receives reliable information that persons affiliated with a foreign ethnic insurgent group intend to use suicide bombers to assassinate that country's president and his entire entourage during an official visit to the United States. Federal law enforcement may appropriately focus investigative attention on identifying members of that ethnic insurgent group who may be present and active in the United States and who, based on other available information, might conceivably be involved in planning some such attack during the state visit.

EIGHT

Racial Profiling Is Not Discriminatory

Walter E. Williams

Racial profiling is not necessarily discriminatory, contends Walter E. Williams in the following selection. Williams argues that while people should not be expressly targeted for their race or ethnicity, valid and useful information can be gleaned from a person's physical appearance. For example, Williams cites several diseases that are more prevalent in certain races; Vietnamese women have been found to experience higher rates of cervical cancer, while black Americans are at special risk for cardiovascular disease. Williams argues it would be wrong for a doctor not to take race into account in this situation, and it likewise is not necessarily discriminatory to do it in other situations as well.

Williams concludes that efforts to profile have more to do with a fear of being robbed than a fear of a particular race. Williams's articles have appeared in *American Economic Review*, *Reader's Digest*, the *Wall Street Journal*, *Newsweek*, and *Capitalism Magazine*, from which this viewpoint was taken. He has also made many TV and radio appearances on such programs as *Firing Line*, *Face the Nation*, *Nightline*, and *Crossfire*.

What is racial profiling, and is it racist? We can think of profiling as using cheap-to-observe characteristics as indicators or proxies for more-costly-to-observe characteristics. A person's physical characteristics, such as race, sex and height, are cheap to observe, and they might be correlated with some other characteristic that's more costly to observe such as disease, strength or ability.

We Profile All the Time

Profiling examples abound. Just knowing that one person is 6 feet 9 inches tall allows one to predict that he's a better basketball player than a 4-feet-9-inch-tall person. That might be called height

Racial Profiling Is Not a Serious Problem

A Massachusetts study found that drivers are stopped in proportion to the racial breakdown of American drivers. For example, the study found that approximately 1.8% of all drivers are Asian, and that Asians are stopped in 1.5% of all traffic stops, indicating stops are made proportionally to the population.

Citations					
Agency	White	Black	Hispanic	Asian	Native American
Average	89.5%	4.1%	4.9%	1.5%	0.1%
Race Disparity	2.8%	-2.3%	-2.3%	0.3%	0.2%

Driving Population Estimate					
Agency	White	Black	Hispanic	Asian	Native American
Average	92.3%	1.7%	2.6%	1.8%	0.3%

Source: Racial Profiling Data Collection, Massachusetts Chiefs of Police Association, May 4, 2004, p.27.

profiling. While height is not a perfect indicator of basketball proficiency, there is a strong association.

Similarly, just knowing the sex or age of an individual allows one to make predictions about unobserved characteristics such as weightlifting ability, running and reflex speed, and eyesight and hearing acuity because they are correlated with sex and age.

Weusi Olusola (l) and Myreo Dixon are both restricted to wheelchairs as a result of violence. Some argue that a high rate of crime among African Americans makes it reasonable for police and others to treat them differently.

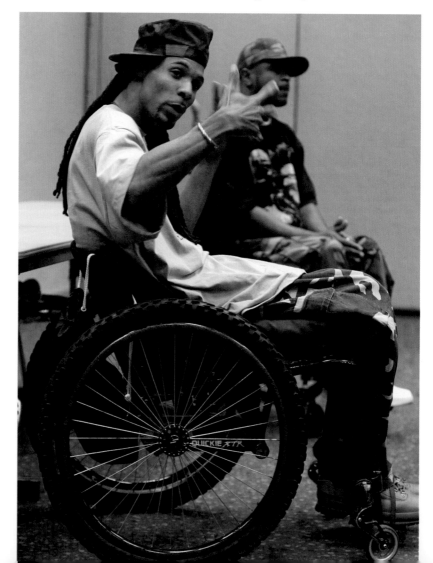

You Can Get Good Information from Race and Ethnicity

What about using race or ethnicity as proxies for some unobserved characteristic? Some racial and ethnic groups have a higher incidence of mortality from various diseases than the national average. In 1998, mortality rates for cardiovascular diseases were approximately 30 percent higher among black adults than among white adults. Cervical cancer rates were almost five times higher among Vietnamese women in the United States than among white women. The Pima Indians of Arizona have the highest known diabetes rates in the world. Prostate cancer is nearly twice as common among black men as white men. Would one condemn a medical practitioner for advising greater screening and monitoring of black males for cardiovascular disease and prostate cancer, or greater screening and monitoring for cervical cancer among Vietnamese American females, and the same for diabetes among Pima Indians? It surely would be racial profiling—using race as an indicator of a higher probability of some other characteristic.

Some Associations Between Race and Crime Are Valid

You might say that's different and that using racial profiling as a proxy for potential criminal behavior is indeed racist. Just as race and ethnicity are not perfect indicators of the risk of certain diseases, neither is race a perfect indicator of criminal activity, but they are associations, and people act on those associations.

A Washington, D.C., taxicab commissioner, who is black, issued a safety advisory urging D.C.'s 6,800 cabbies to refuse to pick up "dangerous looking" passengers. She described "dangerous looking" as a "young black guy . . . with shirttail hanging down longer than his coat, baggy pants, unlaced tennis shoes." By no stretch of imagination does every young black person pose a threat to taxi drivers, but in Washington, D.C., and other cities, there's a strong correlation between race and the threat of robbery/murder.

Profiling Has Its Place

We seriously misunderstand the motives of a taxi driver who passes up a black customer if we use racism as the sole explanation for his behavior. It might be racism, but it might just as easily and more probably be a fear of robbery, murder or being taken to a dangerous neighborhood. There are other examples and greater detail of this phenomenon in my recent *Cornell Law and Public Policy Journal* article "Discrimination: The Law vs. Morality."

Needless to say, the law-abiding black person who's refused a taxi ride or pizza delivery or pulled over by the police is justifiably annoyed and offended. The rightful recipients of his anger should be those blacks who have made black synonymous with high crime and not the taxi driver or pizza deliverer who might fear for his life or the policeman trying to do his job.

By the way, attempting to explain profiling doesn't require one to take a position for or against it any more than attempting to explain gravity requires one to be for or against gravity.

NINE

Racial Profiling Is Good Security

Jens F. Laurson and George Pieler

> Authors Jens F. Laurson and George Pieler argue in the
> following selection that racial profiling makes traveling
> easier and safer for everyone. They contend that although
> it seems unfair to some, a closer look at profiling reveals
> it is the smartest way to keep travelers safe, and does so
> by inconveniencing the fewest number of people. The
> authors urge Americans to stop pretending that politi-
> cians or little old ladies might be terrorists; the war on
> terror involves a very specific group of people who are
> very open about their intentions to harm Americans. For
> these reasons the authors support using racial profiling to
> weed out terrorists.
>
> Laurson is editor in chief of the International Affairs
> Forum. Pieler is senior fellow with the Institute for Policy
> Innovation, from which this viewpoint was taken.

Holiday traffic exposed many glitches in air travel security
as infrequent fliers confronted the ever-changing rules for
carry-on baggage. Despite the United States-European Union
agreement on provisional rules for passenger-data exchange,
air travel security procedures have been up in the air since the

Passengers wait in line at a security checkpoint in Denver's International Airport. Some believe that travel security is more effective and less burdensome for everyone if it is allowed to focus on Middle Eastern and South Asian men.

August [2006] terror plot aimed at the United States and Britain.[1]

Beverages and gels are out, except for 3-ounce travel sizes. Europe's belated decision to allow musicians to travel with their instruments cost renowned Jazz Messengers trumpeter Valery

---

1. In which British Muslims plotted to blow up airlines with liquid explosives.

Ponomarev a broken arm in a tussle with Air India employees in Paris. Most recently, a group of imams were tossed from a US Airways flight after passenger alarm at their loud praying, praising of Allah and unexplained seat changing.

These are excellent reasons to step back and consider the obvious: We should look closely at the passengers boarding each flight. That, alas, leads us into the politically incorrect territory of "ethnic profiling."

We Discriminate Every Single Day

We shy away from any form of "discrimination," yet to discriminate is value neutral: We do it every day in our choices of food, friends and jobs. Government discriminates in deciding what laws and regulations to implement. Security agencies discriminate, focusing their efforts where the yield is greatest. When resources are limited, anything less than prudent discrimination brings waste, demoralization, decreased effectiveness and less security. If, even when lives are at stake, we find flying too burdensome without mascara, water bottles, too-big books and instruments, the answer is common-sense discrimination.

We might wish to treat everyone the same, but the hard truth is we don't (privately or publicly) and shouldn't. For greater flying security, we know to look for Muslim, South Asian/Middle Eastern men. The July 2005 London bombings taught us that the passport matters less than ethnicity—which is just as well, because while passports can be forged, skin color and ethnic features cannot.

Let's Stop Pretending the Terrorists Are All Different Types

It is time we stop pretending that making Al Gore take his shoes off (as happened after Sept. 11) is normal—or that Gore should have to pretend to happily embrace that "egalitarian spirit." The true message of today's airport security measures is that "we are all terrorists now!"

Is it unfair to make men fitting the suicide-terrorist profile "suffer" through extra-strict security measures? Inconveniencing an entire ethnic class for the wrongdoing of a small minority would seem to offend Western values. The truth is, everyone suffers twice when passengers, no matter how low their risk profile, are searched, and everyone is delayed because everyone else is checked. If we simply searched, rigorously, those who constitute even a remote risk based on the history of terror attacks (with apologies, discounts or whatever else might soften the blow of being singled out), even those customers would save time, not having to wait for everyone else to be frisked. Those US Airways imams would have been checked out early and either given a pass or been detained with much less fuss.

Racial Profiling Makes Sense

No one welcomes the implicit accusation of wrongdoing, especially when people to one's left and right do not suffer that indignity. Yet grievances of those designated for greater scrutiny must be weighed against the universal grievance of all travelers. No reasonable passengers today should fail to understand why they have been selected for a more thorough security check. The people so selected might not like it, but the fact is, such checking makes them more secure, too.

Insurance companies use profiling; so does Israel. The history of Western governments profiling for bad motives is disgraceful and explains our trepidation. But we must differentiate between acceptable and unacceptable uses of profiling when civilization and lives are under attack.

Surely we would be outraged if, to prevent drunken-driving deaths, we required every citizen to attend classes against drunken driving. Yet it is imaginable that we might require all those who consume alcohol and have a driver's license to attend. Troubled times call for troubling measures: Let us choose those that inflict the least pain and inconvenience the fewest people.

TEN

Ethnic Team Names Are Discriminatory

Salim Muwakkil

> In the following selection author Salim Muwakkil argues
> that ethnic team names such as the Redskins are discrim-
> inatory. They evoke an ugly past filled with murder, racism,
> and mistreatment, in the author's opinion. Muwakkil is
> surprised that more Americans are not opposed to naming
> their teams after such ugly symbols, and he guesses that
> most either do not think about the meaning the words carry
> or feel entitled to use them on the basis that they did not
> personally participate in genocide against Native
> Americans. Muwakkil urges readers to send these hurtful
> words to the dustbin of history and to name teams after
> symbols all Americans can be proud of.
>
> Muwakkil is a senior editor of *In These Times* and an op-
> ed columnist for the *Chicago Tribune*.

The sports media spoke in a unified voice of praise in January
[2004] when Joe Gibbs was named new coach of the National
Football League's Washington Redskins.

Gibbs is a Hall of Fame coach who led the Washington franchise to three Super Bowl titles in the '80s and '90s. Many headlines enthused his return would mark a "New Era for the Redskins."

Salim Muwakkil, "Racial Slurs Taint U.S. Sports," *Tolerance.org*, April 14, 2004. Copyright ©
2004 In These Times. Reproduced by permission.

The paradox of that idea is striking: In the 21st century an NFL team is still known by an ethnic slur crafted during the nation's frontier days.

Our Team Names Evoke Genocide and Racism

The term "Redskins" derives from an old, genocidal practice in this country of scalping Native Americans to earn a bounty. A bounty hunter could prove he had killed a native by turning in a scalp,

A fan of the Cleveland Indians holds up a sign bearing the Indians' mascot, Chief Wahoo, before a 1997 playoff game against the New York Yankees.

which often were bloody and called "redskins." This bit of etymology was part of a July 2000 editorial in Maine's *Portland Press Herald* explaining why it banned the team name from its sports pages.

But in *The Washington Post* there were few questions raised about coupling the team's new era with a racist slur from an old era. This newspaper that serves the "capital of the free world" still prints that insult in bold headlines.

Americans Should Be Outraged

It may be true that stereotyping nonwhites is as American as apple pie, and such deeply ingrained cultural habits die hard, but the lack of public outrage at these continuing racial slurs is a bit surprising. After all, there's little debate that the use of people as mascots is, at best, humiliating.

As the American Jewish Committee noted in a 1998 report, "The use of mascots is a reflection of the limits of dehumanization our culture will allow."

The name of the D.C. NFL franchise is particularly egregious, but it is far from the lone offender among professional sports teams.

The Cleveland Indians and their "Chief Wahoo," is another, as are the Kansas City Chiefs and the Atlanta Braves. Universities, like North Dakota, Illinois and Florida State among others still sport Native American mascots.

Slowly Making Gains

But there is increasing opposition, as well. Other newspapers have banished Native symbols and logos from their pages. *The Lincoln Journal Star* in Nebraska has banned the Redskins name and has stopped printing logos for professional and college sports teams that use or caricature Native American symbols. *The Oregonian*, the Minnesota *St. Cloud Times*, the Minneapolis *Star Tribune* and *The Kansas City Star* also limit publication of Native mascots and images in varying ways.

Many colleges and universities across the country have dropped their Native American mascots, and some schools, like the University of Minnesota, won't compete with out-of-conference schools that use Native American mascots, names or logos. Several public school systems, including those of Dallas and Los Angeles, also prohibit the use of such symbols.

Despite Opposition, Americans Are Drawn to Hurtful Names

Virtually every Native American organization has condemned the use of demeaning images or mascots. In 2003, the Native American Journalists Association urged news organizations to stop using sports mascots and nicknames that depict Native Americans by 2004.

Yet, many Americans seem to believe that their right to use these symbols in frivolous, casual ways is a matter of personal opinion. Had some reporter interrupted the Gibbs veneration fest with a question about the Redskin name, it would have been dismissed as so much political correctness.

Discard the Stereotypes

The fight against Native American mascots and logos is a serious struggle to overturn the stereotypes and cultural assumptions that were forged in our racist past but still help determine the trajectories of our lives today.

And while more Americans are becoming aware of this struggle to rearrange our cultural iconography, resistance remains strong.

The offense of anti-black images like "Black Sambo," or anti-Latino ones like the "Frito Bandito" only recently have been made obvious to many Americans, and we still find it difficult to understand why Native Americans find sports symbols demeaning.

Like those Redskins fans who insist their team's name is an honorable tribute, partisans of mascots everywhere claim their devotion is bias-free.

Let's Send Racist Team Names to the Dustbin of History

Americans' denial of indigenous peoples' grievances is a product of our sordid role in their history. Americans stole their lands,

Bob Englehart, *The Hartford Courant,* and PoliticalCartoons.com.

destroyed their civilizations and damned near killed off all their people. That's a lot of baggage to carry; why not deny?

What I find mystifying, however, is the civil rights community's lack of attention to this issue. One would shudder to think what the NAACP would do with a sports team named the Chicago Jigaboos. We saw how angry many black groups became when the rapper Nelly announced he was marketing something called "Pimp Juice." African Americans know the difficulty of holding America accountable for the errors of its past, so we should be leading the way in correcting the ongoing error of demeaning mascots.

That's why I was happy to see Bill Fletcher Jr. of TransAfrica Forum make the call for other black groups to get involved in the fight to change the name of the Washington Redskins. I join Fletcher in his call and expand it to retire all Native American mascots to the dustbin of discarded stereotypes.

ELEVEN

Ethnic Team Names Are Not Discriminatory

Andrew Cline

> In the following selection author Andrew Cline argues that ethnic team names are not discriminatory. He writes in response to the National Collegiate Athletic Association's decision to ban eighteen university and college team nicknames it found discriminatory to Native Americans. Cline argues the NCAA's decision is arbitrary because it attacks some ethnic names, such as the use of the tribal name "Illini," but allows others, such as "Dakota." Furthermore, the author argues that naming teams after Native Americans and other ethnic groups is often a compliment. Names such as "Vikings," "Seminoles," and "Sioux" conjure up images of heroes, strength, and bravery, he believes. Cline concludes by arguing that many Native Americans support the use of tribal references in team names, and thus they should be allowed to be used.
>
> Cline is editorial page editor of the *New Hampshire Union Leader* and a regular contributor to the *Spectator*, from which this viewpoint was taken.

The National Collegiate Athletic Association's executive committee—comprised of 14 white men, two white women, and three black men—decided last week that 18 university and college nicknames were "hostile and abusive" to Indians. The nicknames and mascots may not be displayed on any team uniform at any NCAA postseason tournament starting next February. It was a new milestone in condescending liberal racism.

If Native Americans Don't Mind, Why Should Others?

The committee members were the sole arbiters of what was "hostile and abusive" and what was not. Among those not allowed a say in the matter were, ahem, Indians.

After NCAA busybodies spent time snooping around Tallahassee, Florida, to gather evidence for their case against Florida State's use of the Seminoles nickname, the Seminole Tribal Council voted in April [2005]—unanimously—to affirm the tribe's support for the university's nickname and mascot. Nonetheless, come August [2005]

Max B. Osceola (left) of the Seminole Tribal Council presents gifts to Florida State University president T.K. Wetherell. The gifts symbolize the tribe's support for FSU's use of "Seminoles" as the nickname for its sports teams.

the NCAA decreed FSU's use of the name "hostile and abusive." Those silly Indians, they obviously don't know what's good for them.

Also banned is the nickname of the University of Illinois—the Illini. "Illini" was the name of the tribal confederation that once ruled the land now called Illinois. It is the root word for the state name and the name of its people, Illinoians. It is hard to see hostility in a name the white people use to describe themselves, but the NCAA sees it.

University of Illinois basketball jerseys say "Illinois," not "Illini." In its eternal wisdom, the executive committee will allow jerseys printed with "Illinois," but not ones printed with "Illini." What will committee members do when they learn that "Illinois" is French for "Illini"?

Multicultural Sensitivity Can Go Too Far

Allowing jerseys to bear the French name for the Illini tribal confederation, but not the name the confederation gave itself, is the logical end point of multicultural sensitivity. One wonders whether the University of Illinois student newspaper—*The Illini*—will be allowed to cover future NCAA tournaments.

Bob Englehart, *The Hartford Courant*, and PoliticalCartoons.com.

Indiana University, whose athletic teams are called "Hoosiers," escaped the NCAA's nickname ban. But Indiana's jerseys don't say "Hoosiers." They say "Indiana," which means "Land of Indians."

By the way, the NCAA is headquartered in Indianapolis—"City of the Land of Indians." How embarrassing.

The NCAA has banned the University of North Dakota's "Fighting Sioux" nickname. "Sioux" is the name for a confederation of smaller tribes, including the Dakota. If UND removes the "hostile and abusive" "Sioux" name from its jerseys and replaces it with "North Dakota," it will still have a tribal name on its jerseys. Obviously, the NCAA executives have not thought their plan through.

Most Names Refer to Something Else

The University of Oklahama's football team wears jerseys sporting the university's team nickname: Sooners. Sooners were people who illegally occupied land confiscated from the Indians. (They got there "sooner" than the law allowed.) The university's basketball team wears jerseys bearing the state name: Oklahoma. "Oklahoma" is Choctaw for "red people." Both of these names are OK, while "Seminoles," approved by the tribe, is banned. Go figure.

A thought to consider: If [basketball player] Cherokee Parks becomes a college basketball coach, or [actress] Dakota Fanning plays a varsity sport in 2012, will announcers be permitted to mention their names on air?

A college referee I know wonders whether Billy Packer and Greg Gumbel will be allowed to say "Fighting Sioux" or "Seminoles." Play-by-play certainly will be clumsy if nicknames cannot be used.

Ethnic and Historic Names Are Not Racist

All of this nonsense is born of the notion that when white people adopt the name and likeness of red people, it is an act of racism, an assertion of racial or tribal superiority. After all, the University of North Carolina at Pembroke, a historically Indian institution, was allowed to keep its "Braves" nickname. Yet white people usually are not being condescending by adopting Indian names or mascots.

Athletic teams wish to associate themselves with qualities valued on the field of play: courage, valor, strength, endurance, bravery. Hence they choose names and mascots they believe emblematic of those qualities: Sioux, Vikings, Seminoles, Celtics, Bears, Tigers, Yankees, Pirates, etc. No one names his team the Pigeons.

To the NCAA executive committee, unencumbered by reality, the actual intent behind the nickname's adoption does not matter. All that matters is how others might perceive it.

Let's Reject Racist Paternalism

The best reaction to this fear of offense, of course, is to let individual institutions work out these disagreements on their own. Instead, the paternalism that comes from intellectual superiority has overruled common sense. And so 19 white and black university and college executives have told countless Indians what is best for them. It is the very definition of racist paternalism.

I hope each of the 18 institutions affected by this policy makes every NCAA tournament next year. And I hope they wear their uniforms, unaltered, and force the NCAA to drag their players off the courts, fields, tracks and mats. Bureaucratic bullying is easy when it can be done with the stroke of a pen. When it has to be backed up by brute force, it becomes a lot more difficult to justify.

TWELVE

Banning Gay Marriage Is Discrimination

Steve Trussell and Elizabeth Schulte

Steve Trussell and Elizabeth Schulte argue in the following selection that banning gay marriage is discrimination against gays and lesbians. They liken the struggle to legalize gay marriage to the struggle for racial equality in the 1960s and the suffragist struggle in the early twentieth century for women's rights. Prohibiting people from marrying based on their sexual orientation is a violation of their civil rights, claim the authors, and reduces them to second class citizens in much the same way blacks were forced to ride at the back of buses and drink from separate water fountains in previous eras. Trussell and Schulte reject efforts to adopt a constitutional amendment banning gay marriage, arguing that bigotry and discrimination should not be enshrined in the document that is supposed to protect the freedoms and rights of all Americans, gay or straight.

Trussell and Schulte are reporters for the *Socialist Worker*, from which this viewpoint was taken.

Same-sex couples across Massachusetts will gather at county clerk's offices to apply for marriage licenses on May 17 [2004]. They are likely to get them—making Massachusetts the first state in U.S. history to issue legal licenses to gay and lesbian couples.

Steve Trussell and Elizabeth Schulte, "Why Gay Marriage Is a Civil Right," *Socialist Worker Online*, May 14, 2004, p. 5. Reproduced by permission.

On Monday, a court-mandated 180-day waiting period will end, and the state government is under orders from the Massachusetts Supreme Judicial Court to grant the licenses—as a result of its landmark *Goodridge* decision last year. But as *Socialist Worker* goes to press a week before the deadline, groups of state lawmakers and religious organizations were hoping to win court injunctions to block the licenses from being issued—on the grounds that the Court overstepped its bounds in its ruling.

The Legal Battle over Gay Marriage

Gay rights activists and their supporters hope that if and when gay marriages become reality in Massachusetts, they will be hard to take away—even though a constitutional amendment to ban same-sex marriage, supported by both Republicans and Democrats, is in the works. People across the state will attend or know about same-sex marriage ceremonies in the coming months—giving increased visibility to gay and lesbian families that will likely win broader support for the cause of equal rights.

It's also likely to add to the backlash—from the bigots who want to turn back the clock. Ever since the Supreme Judicial Court ruled in favor of gay marriage in November [2003], antigay politicians have worked tirelessly to block the licenses.

Gov. Mitt Romney is continuing his attempts to win a stay of the ruling—to avoid "legal confusion" as the state legislature moves forward with a proposed amendment to the state constitution defining marriage as between "one man and one woman." At the very least, state officials are under Romney's instructions to enforce a 1913 law designed to prevent interracial marriages—by denying licenses to couples from out of state.

Massachusetts activists for gay marriage have relied on a purely legal strategy to defend the *Goodridge* decision. Many see the approach of May 17 without the right [of] stopping same-sex marriage as proof that a legal strategy alone can win civil rights. But this attitude has slowed the momentum of the gay marriage movement nationally—and is holding it back in many places.

Obstacles and Delays

In March [2004], the California Supreme Court stopped San Francisco from issuing marriage licenses to gay and lesbian couples. When Mayor Gavin Newsom agreed to abide by the decision, gays and lesbians took his lead by agreeing to let the legal process play out.

In Rhode Island—next to Massachusetts, with no laws banning gay marriage and many openly gay officials—efforts to demand equal marriage rights have been silenced by "gay-friendly" politicians. There is every reason to see Rhode Island as the next battleground in the gay marriage struggle. Yet state Sen. Rhoda Perry, who sponsored gay marriage legislation, isn't calling for a vote on the measure. "We think its best not to do anything this year," Perry said.

In Massachusetts, those who advocate the legal road have played down setbacks and refused to admit defeats—as when the state legislature took the first steps toward passing a constitutional ban on gay marriage earlier this year. Last week, the New Hampshire House of Representatives passed a measure that bars recognition of marriage licenses obtained by same-sex couples in other states.

Advocates for Gay Marriage Cannot Rely on Democrats to Defend Gays' Right to Marry

The fact remains that 38 states in the U.S. prohibit gay marriage—and 13 states are pursuing constitutional bans. Yet in the face of this backlash, most supporters of gay marriage have been content to put their faith in Democratic Party politicians.

This is a recipe for defeat. Out of 273 Democrats in Congress, only seven have publicly spoken in favor of gay marriage. When Massachusetts Sen. John Kerry—the Democrats' certain presidential nominee—was asked to comment on Romney's use of the 1913 segregation law, he had no comment.

The Democratic Party's establishment won't publicly support real equality for gays and lesbians. It can't be trusted with the future of this struggle for our rights. In fact, the party's leadership seems to have temporarily regained control of the situation, successfully

Well-wishers shower a same-sex couple with rice as they emerge from the Northampton, Massachusetts, municipal offices with marriage license in hand.

reeling in the likes of Newsom and redirecting the efforts of gay rights organizations into purely legal channels.

End Marriage Discrimination Now

All this shows why a legal strategy—while important—can't win gay marriage by itself. We need a grassroots movement that fights for broad support—and makes it impossible for the politicians to continue treating gays, lesbians, bisexuals and transgendered as second-class citizens.

May 17 is not only the day that Massachusetts is supposed to end marriage discrimination. It is also the 50th anniversary of the *Brown v. Board of Education* decision that outlawed racial segregation in public schools. Activists should remember that the *Brown* decision marked the *beginning* of a new phase in the civil rights struggle that ended segregation—not the end.

Gays and Lesbians Are Treated Like Second-Class Citizens

The outpouring of support for gay marriage came on the scene like a lightning bolt. Couples lined up in the thousands on the courthouse steps in San Francisco after Mayor Gavin Newsom announced that same-sex marriage licenses would be issued beginning February 12 [2004]. The lines didn't thin out, either—until March 12, when the state Supreme Court ruled that the city had to stop issuing the licenses.

In cities large and small—from Portland, Ore., to Sandoval County, N.M.—local officials began issuing same-sex marriage licenses. New Paltz, N.Y. Mayor Jason West of the Green Party issued licenses in open defiance of state laws. And in cities across the country, gay rights supporters organized protests to demand marriage rights.

In a matter of weeks, there was finally a platform for people to express their outrage at the right-wing's attempts to relegate gay, lesbian, bisexual and transgender (GLBT) people to second-class citizenship—and to confidently demand full and equal rights. All this was largely set in motion by the expectations raised by the Massachusetts Supreme Judicial Court's decisions on gay marriage, which declared that "separate is seldom, if ever, equal."

Don't Put Discrimination in the Constitution

More people still were mobilized when George W. Bush announced in February [2004] that he would support an amendment to the federal constitution banning gay marriage. Like the Southern bigots who opposed integrated schools and interracial marriage, the antigay Christian Right also took action. Groups like the Campaign for California Families—with legal teams and money to burn— tried to pass state gay marriage bans.

These mostly white groups want to take advantage of the conservatism of some minority, especially African American, churches on the issue of gay rights. For example, in March, Genevieve Wood of the antigay Family Research Council, warned a group of Black evangelical ministers that gays "are wrapping themselves in the flag of civil rights. I can make arguments against that. But not nearly like you all can."

But not many African Americans bought the bigots' claims. In Georgia, Black religious leaders in the state House of Representatives cast the deciding votes that temporarily stopped a proposed constitutional ban on gay marriage. "What I see in this is hate," state Rep. Georganna Sinkfield told the *New York Times*, "I'm a Christian, but if we put this in the Constitution, what's next? People with dark hair? You're opening the floodgates for people to promote their own prejudice."

Gay Marriage Is a Civil Rights Issue

The right of gays and lesbians to marry is a civil rights issue—every bit as much as Jim Crow segregation or voting rights in the racist South. As Cynthia Rickert told the *San Francisco Chronicle* after she and her partner were married in February [2004], "Everybody has a right to love each other. It's time for us to get off the back of the bus." There can be no compromise on this point.

Democratic politicians have urged patience on the issue of marriage, backing civil unions instead. But not only do the rights granted under civil unions fall far short of marriage—such as access to spousal Social Security benefits—but the distinction also leaves gays with a separate and unequal status. Gay, lesbian, bisexual and transgender couples deserve the same rights as anybody else, period.

This should be our message to "gay-friendly" Democratic politicians who coach patience or compromise—like openly gay Rep. Barney Frank (D-Mass.), who urged Gavin Newsom to stop issuing same-sex marriage licenses. "I was sorry to see the San Francisco thing go forward," Frank told the Associated Press in February. "When you're in a real struggle, San Francisco making a symbolic point becomes a diversion."

For Democrats like Frank, the "real struggle" is in getting John Kerry[1] elected in November—and so he wants activists to delay their fight so that a Democrat who *opposes* gay marriage can take the White House. We can't let the politicians turn the fight for equal marriage on and off like a spigot when it suits them.

There is no shortcut. Only building activist organizations and actions that put pressure on the politicians can guarantee that gays and lesbians will win equal rights—without compromises. This will be the key to the struggles for gay marriage that lie ahead.

1. John Kerry ran for president in November 2004 but lost.

THIRTEEN

Banning Gay Marriage Is Not Discrimination

Eugene F. Rivers and Kenneth D. Johnson

In the following selection authors Eugene F. Rivers and Kenneth D. Johnson argue that banning gay marriage does not constitute discrimination because it is not a violation of rights. Gay Americans are not denied anything that straight Americans have —they are allowed to marry, just not someone of the same sex. The authors point out that comparisons to the black civil rights movement of the 1960s are invalid because blacks sought to achieve the same rights, freedoms, and services extended to white Americans. Such institutions are already extended to gay Americans, whether or not they choose to take advantage of them as they exist. In the authors' opinions, preferences and desires—such as sexal orientation—do not constitute rights, and thus banning gay marriage does not count as discriminatory.

Rivers is founder and president of the Seymour Institute for Advanced Christian Studies and is a pastor of the Church of God in Christ, the nation's largest historically black Pentecostal denomination. Johnson is the senior fellow for social policy and civil society at the Seymour Institute for Advanced Christian Studies.

The movement to redefine marriage to include same-sex unions has packaged its demands in the rhetoric and images of the civil rights movement. This strategy, though cynical, has enormous strategic utility. For what reasonable, fair-minded American could object to a movement that conjures up images of Martin Luther King Jr. and his fellow campaigners for racial justice facing down dogs and fire hoses? Who is prepared to risk being labeled a bigot for opposing same-sex marriage?

Applying the "Race Card" to Gay Marriage

As an exercise in marketing and merchandising, this strategy is the most brilliant playing of the race card in recent memory. Not since the "poverty pimps" of 35 years ago, who leveraged the guilt and sense of fair play of the American public to hustle affirmative action set-asides, have we witnessed so brazen a misuse of African-American history for partisan purposes.

But the partisans of homosexual marriage have a problem. There is no evidence in the history and literature of the civil rights movement, or in its genesis in the struggle against slavery, to support the claim that the "gay rights" movement is in the tradition of the African-American struggle for civil rights. As the eminent historian Eugene D. Genovese observed more than 30 years ago, the black American experience as a function of slavery is unique and without analogue in the history of the United States. While other ethnic and social groups have experienced discrimination and hardship, none of their experiences compare with the physical and cultural brutality of slavery. It was in the crucible of the unique experience of slavery that the civil rights movement was born.

Exploiting History

The extraordinary history of the United States as a slaveholding republic included the kidnapping and brutal transport of blacks from African shores, and the stripping of their language, identity, and culture in order to subjugate and exploit them. It also included the constitutional enshrining of these evils in the form of a Supreme Court decision—*Dred Scott v. Sandford*—denying

Opponents of same-sex marriage argue that by its very nature, marriage can only take place between a man and a woman.

to blacks any rights that whites must respect, and the establishment of Jim Crow and *de jure* racial discrimination after *Dred Scott* was overturned by a civil war and three historic constitutional amendments.

It is these basic facts that embarrass efforts to exploit the rhetoric of civil rights to advance the goals of generally privileged groups, however much they wish to depict themselves as victims. Whatever wrongs individuals have suffered because some Americans fail in the basic moral obligation to love the sinner, even while hating the sin, there has never been an effort to create a subordinate class subject to exploitation based on "sexual orientation."

Desires and Preferences Are Not Rights

It is precisely the indiscriminate promotion of various social groups' *desires and preferences as* "rights" that has drained the moral authority from the civil rights industry. Let us consider the question of rights. What makes a gay activist's aspiration to overturn thousands of years of universally recognized morality and practice a "right"? Why should an institution designed for the reproduction of civil society and the rearing of children in a moral environment in which their interests are given pride of place be refashioned to accommodate relationships integrated around intrinsically non-marital sexual conduct?

One must, in the current discussion, address directly the assertion of discrimination. The claim that the definition of marriage as the union of one man and one woman constitutes discrimination is based on a false analogy with statutory prohibitions on interracial marriages in many states through much of the 20th century. This alleged analogy collapses when one considers that skin pigmentation is utterly irrelevant to the procreative and unitive functions of marriage. Racial differences do not interfere with the ability of sexually complementary spouses to become "one-flesh," as the Book of Genesis puts it, by sexual intercourse that fulfills the behavioral conditions of procreation. As the law of marital consummation makes clear, and always has made clear, it is this bodily union that serves as the foundation of the profound sharing of life at every level—biological, emotional, dispositional, rational, and spiritual—that marriage is. This explains not only why marriage can only be between a man and a woman, but also why marriages cannot be between more than two people—despite the desire of "polyamorists" to have their sexual preferences and practices legally recognized and blessed.

Prohibiting Gay Marriage Does Not Violate Any "Right"

Moreover, the analogy of same-sex marriage to interracial marriage disregards the whole point of those prohibitions, which was to maintain and advance a system of racial subordination and exploitation. It was to maintain a caste system in which one race was relegated to conditions of social and economic inferiority. The definition of marriage as the union of a man and a woman does not establish a sexual caste system or relegate one sex to conditions of social and economic inferiority. It does, to be sure, deny the recognition as lawful "marriages" to some forms of sexual combining—including polygyny, polyandry, polyamory, and same-sex relationships. But there is nothing invidious or discriminatory about laws that decline to treat all sexual wants or proclivities as equal.

People are equal in worth and dignity, but *sexual choices* and lifestyles are not. That is why the law's refusal to license polygamous, polyamorous, and homosexual unions is entirely right and proper. In recognizing, favoring, and promoting traditional, monogamous marriage, the law does not violate the "rights" of people whose "lifestyle preferences" are denied the stamp of legal approval. Rather, it furthers and fosters the common good of civil society, and makes proper provision for the physical and moral protection and nurturing of children.

Stop Hijacking the Civil Rights Legacy

Well-intentioned liberals shudder upon hearing the word "discrimination." Its simple enunciation instills guilt and dulls their critical faculties. But once malcontented members of any group—however privileged—can simply invoke the term and launch their own personalized civil rights industry, the word has been emptied of its normative and historical content.

Defending the civil rights legacy should prove cold comfort to its historic advocates, because the loss of its distinctive nature is our own fault. It was our failure, philosophically and politically, to develop a compelling historiography of the movement that contributed to its decline and decay. From the teaching in schools, to the use of the phrase in political discourse, the notion of civil rights has been diluted, ahistoricized, and nearly emptied of content in relation to the lived historical experience of black Americans.

It is especially sad and disturbing that many self-proclaimed civil rights leaders have failed to resist corruption and co-optation by the homosexual movement. People who should be vitally concerned with promoting marriage and rebuilding the institution of marriage in African-American communities are either silent or complicit in a campaign which, if successful, will trivialize marriage.

We Need an Amendment to Protect Marriage

In light of the prospect of judicially mandated homosexual marriage, we believe that black leaders—and especially black

Banning Gay Marriage in the Constitution

According to a 2005 Gallup poll, Americans continually favor adopting a constitutional amendment that would ban gay marriage, indicating they do not believe gay marriage is a civil rights issue.

Would you favor or oppose a constitutional amendment that would define marriage as being between a man and a woman, thus barring marriages between gay or lesbian couples?

Date	Favor	Oppose	Other
March 2005	57%	37%	6%
July 2004	48%	47%	5%
May 2004	51%	45%	4%
March 2004	50%	45%	4%
February 2004(b)	52%	45%	3%
February 2004(a)	49%	46%	5%
July 2003	50%	45%	5%

Source: Joshua K. Baker, "Same-Sex Marriage: Recent Trends in Public Opinion," Institute for Marriage and Public Policy, April 29, 2005.

clergy—need to speak forcefully in favor of President George W. Bush's proposal for a Federal Marriage Amendment. If their support for true marriage alienates them from their white liberal friends, so be it. No community has suffered more than has ours from the weakening of the institution of marriage at the hands of purveyors of the doctrines of the sexual revolution. It is our sons and our daughters who have paid the costs imposed by a cultural elite that seeks to overthrow cultural and Biblical principles of sexual restraint and responsibility. Leaders of our community should therefore be in the vanguard of the movement to prevent further moral erosion and begin reversing historical declines.

FOURTEEN

Race-Based Humor Goes Too Far

David Edelstein

In the following selection writer David Edelstein discusses race-based humor, such as the television shows *South Park*, *Curb Your Enthusiasm*, and the movie *Borat: Cultural Learnings of America for Make Benefit Glorious Nation of Kazakhstan*. He argues that although these shows and movies get a lot of laughs from anti-Semitic, antigay, and other discriminatory humor, such joking can go too far and is a cheap way to entertain audiences. Edelstein describes how he cringes during such routines because even though they are supposed to be funny, he finds them depressing and believes they reinforce discriminatory ideas that society has worked hard to eradicate. He concludes that although racial humor has its place, the type that is currently popular is so overt it is almost horrific to watch.

Edelstein is a writer for *New York Magazine*, from which this viewpoint was taken.

Most clowns have a wide streak of sadism, but it's tempting to think of [actor] Sacha Baron Cohen as a sadist with a wide streak of clownishness. In *Borat* (full title: *Borat: Cultural Learnings of America for Make Benefit Glorious Nation of Kazakhstan*), Baron Cohen embodies a Kazakh television journalist—a character he created for his HBO series, *Da Ali G Show*—who embarks on a cross-country American odyssey in the hopes of learning the Westerners' secrets of civilization. A beanpole with a black Stalin brush mustache and a look of genial befuddlement, Borat poses earnest questions to his subjects that betray his minuscule IQ, cultural backwardness, rampant libido, sexism, homophobia, and anti-Semitism. His clueless American interviewees-victims—actual people who think an actual Kazakh is actually quizzing them—do their best to tutor him in Our Ways, patiently explaining the etiquette of dating and dining, the underlying tenets of feminism, the fine points of law enforcement. When Borat, in his good-natured, upbeat way, says something grossly inappropriate about women or Jews, they attempt to overlook it: They understand that he's from the Third World, that his grasp of our language and mores is shaky. We laugh at them for thinking that they are superior to him—for their noblesse oblige. We laugh at them when they let his outlandish interjections pass, and we laugh at them when they become visibly uptight. We laugh at them when they take offense, and we laugh at them when—like a group of frat-house slobs who give him a ride in their RV—they take no offense whatsoever. I stopped laughing when, at a formal southern dinner party with several older couples, Borat announced that two of the ladies would be considered very desirable in his country, then gestured to the plainer woman at the far end of the table and said, "Her, not so much." As the preview audience roared, I put my head down; I didn't want to see the face of that poor woman. And at that point, I guess, the joke was on me.

Race-Based Humor Is Painful

Underlying the above account is not a plea for a more civilized, courteous, or comfortable kind of comedy. Screw that. The comic imagination flowers on the dark-and-twisted end of the spectrum; in return for making you laugh, the artist has license to express rude truths in the rudest manner he or she can imagine. With her pipeline to the id of the solipsistic American female, Sarah Silverman [an actress known for her tasteless racial humor] generates breathtaking geysers of tastelessness. Television's most trench-

Sacha Baron Cohen appears in character as Borat Sagdiyev at the MTV Europe Music Awards ceremony.

ant satire is *South Park*. If you're in the right, juvenile frame of mind, *Jackass Number Two*, a set of absurdly perilous stunts and practical jokes, can leave you exhausted from cackling and screaming simultaneously at a posse of overgrown 10-year-olds driven to push the boundaries of sense.

No, this is a cry of pain. As someone with an admittedly low tolerance for watching the humiliation of others—I find it hard to look at the faces of baseball players after they've struck out—I'm spending more and more time squirming, cringing, averting my eyes, and plugging my ears. It's worse, obviously, when real people are getting burned—although on something like *American Idol* the contestants at least know what they're in for. But even fictional works are becoming harder to endure. In both its British and American incarnations, *The Office* revolves around the relentless degradation of a cretinous middle manager who's desperate to be liked. Its brilliant creator, Ricky Gervais, now plumbs the depths of his (apparent) self-hatred on *Extras*. *Curb Your Enthusiasm* requires you to identify with a man who shrinks might say has a narcissistic personality disorder, and whose sense of entitlement has a way of escalating the most casual negotiations of modern society into appalling confrontations. And we're not talking about one scene per episode. It's virtually every scene.

Gasping at Outlandish Racial Humor

The squirm-und-drang genre has its forebears, among them Albert Brooks, but I would guess that it has caught on now because it's grounded in a documentary (or mockumentary) aesthetic. As the jittery handheld camera has found a place in even the slickest

Sandy Huffaker and PoliticalCartoons.com.

commercial concoctions, audiences have developed an appetite for the sting of reality: real time, real pain. Not just liveness—live-wireness.

The Sultan of Squirm is surely Baron Cohen, a sublime caricaturist whose hairbreadth timing can make you gasp. As Ali G, whose black-rapper gesticulations border on Kabuki, he asks his (frequently right-wing) guests questions of such overbearing idiocy that he often shuts them down completely (a victory of sorts in this genre). But it's his Borat who has the more righteously malicious agenda.

Racial Humor Spares No One—Not Even the Joker

To understand what Baron Cohen's Borat is up to in part, it helps to consider the most notorious scenes in Claude Lanzmann's nine-and-a-half-hour Holocaust documentary, *Shoah*, in which the director trains his camera on Polish peasants who lived near the Nazis' most lethal concentration camps while they were in full swing. Under Lanzmann's probing, these old men and women—some of them residing on property seized from the Jews—murmur that yes, it was a terrible thing, the exterminations. Just terrible. But of course, the Jews did bring it on themselves, didn't they? I don't know whether Baron Cohen saw *Shoah*, but Lanzmann's gotcha journalism on untutored anti-Semites paved the way for what amounts to a (riotous) libel on Eastern Europe.

Baron Cohen grew up in an Orthodox Jewish home, speaks fluent Hebrew, and came of age with the punks and then the rappers. Several years ago, he met a doctor in the south of Russia whom he described (on the DVD of *Da Ali G Show*'s first season) as unintentionally hilarious. Now he identifies with the anti-Semite aggressor for the purposes of travestying him. The film begins in a small town in Kazakhstan—incestuous, inbred, where the local rapist is regarded as a colorful eccentric ("naughty, naughty") and every year the citizens have the "running of the Jew" in which the masked, demonic figure attempts to "get the money." For the role, Baron Cohen didn't use deodorant or wash his one ugly pale-blue suit—so when he got in close to his subjects, they had to contend with his stench along with his stupidity. And so Borat spares no one: not the interviewees, not the interviewer.

Depressing to Watch, Painful to Laugh At

I loved Borat in small doses on the TV show—his deferential affect was a nice change of tune after Ali G's belligerence. But except for a screamingly funny climax in which he attempts to kidnap Pamela Anderson (who reportedly wasn't in on the joke), I found the Borat feature (directed by Larry Charles, who does similar duties on *Curb Your Enthusiasm*) depressing; and the paroxysms of the audience reinforced the feeling that I was watching a bearbaiting or pigsticking. Baron Cohen is such an inspired comic actor that it's a little disappointing when he jumps so quickly, so eagerly to offend the people he interviews; it would be more fun, I think, if he gave them some room to maneuver. But then, of course, we wouldn't squirm or cringe. And then comedy wouldn't be evolving in the way it is now—to the point that it bleeds into horror.

FIFTEEN

Race-Based Humor Helps Us Overcome Racial Issues

Pike Wright

> Race-based humor such as that delivered by comedians Sarah Silverman, Sacha Baron Cohen, and Dave Chappelle can help Americans overcome racial issues, argues Pike Wright in the following selection. She discusses how comedians increasingly rely on race-based humor to get laughs, yet carefully monitor their content and delivery so that racists are the butt of the joke. Modern comedy has turned racial quandaries upside down and makes it clear why racism is so ridiculous in the first place. Wright concludes that race-based humor can go a long way in helping Americans improve their dialogue on racial issues.
>
> Wright is a journalist and poet living in Toronto, Ontario, Canada. She writes for various activist magazines including *This Magazine*, from which this viewpoint was taken.

Most celebrities simply walk down the red carpet of the Toronto International Film Festival. Not so Borat Sagdiyev: At his feature film debut, the "Kazakh reporter" (played by British comedian Sacha Baron Cohen) arrived in an ox cart pulled by actors dressed as peasant women in headscarves. He flashed two thumbs up, consciously imitating the quintessentially American gesture. The antics were obviously a reference to what Borat claims is a Kazakh saying: "In my country they say, 'God, then man, then horse, then dog, then woman, then rat.'" The crowd, whose numbers rivaled those for any Hollywood celebrity at the festival, loved it, cheering him on.

Borat: Cultural Learnings of America for Make Benefit Glorious Nation of Kazakhstan—which opened to packed theatres and rave reviews across North America in November 2006—is ostensibly a state-sponsored documentary for Kazakhs to learn about American culture. The film builds upon Borat's previous appearances on HBO's comedy *Da Ali G Show*. A hit in Britain, in North America Borat continues to be wildly popular, to the ire of the Kazakhstan government, which has long fought his misogynist, anti-Semitic and racist portrayal of Kazakh culture. (Though it appears the government has finally got the joke; Kazakhstan's culture and information minister recently called the film "funny," acknowledging that Americans are its real target.)

Race-Based Humor Is Increasingly Popular

Nothing-is-sacred comedians like Cohen have long explored these issues through parody, especially as discussions about stereotypes become more taboo in polite conversation. The popularity of comedians such as Margaret Cho, Dave Chappelle, Sarah Silverman and Canada's Russell Peters reflects the fact that questions of difference, particularly race and cultural difference, fascinate us. Their acts are charged with ethnic humour about their own communities and others that is sure to offend. But is it racist?

While we can measure the immediate success of a joke by the laughter or catcalls it provokes, we can also consider the spontaneous reaction that a joke provokes as indicative of a deeper emotional landscape. Whether we find a joke funny, dirty, racist or just dumb depends on who is telling the joke, and to whom, especially when a comedian is parodying a racist character.

Racial Humor Is Not Necessarily Racist

In Borat's case, the joke is that he isn't really an anti-Semite. Cohen, his creator, describes himself as an observant Jew. Talking

Sarah Silverman appears at the 2007 Spirit Awards.

to everyday Americans about patriotism, hunting, politics and dating, Borat's enthusiastic curiosity, coupled with a dose of stupidity, makes his misogyny and anti-Semitism excusable—he is just a foreigner, after all, with different beliefs that must be tolerated. His ignorance of the inappropriateness of discussing the sexual prowess of his sister or asking how to defend himself against the "Jew claw attack" endears him to his fans.

In one episode of *Da Ali G Show*, Borat convinces a roomful of country-western fans in Tucson, Arizona, to sing along with a fabricated Kazakh ditty, singing "Throw the Jew down the well / So my country can be free. / You must grab him by his horns, / Then we have a big party." The audience indulges him, shouting back the chorus and tapping along to the beat, unaware that they've been had.

Of course, it is no longer acceptable for comedians or other public figures to take up explicitly racist attitudes—the days of blackface, George Carlin and Andrew Dice Clay are retreating. But racism isn't. So Cohen uses the bumbling Borat to give voice to racist sentiment. Black comedian Dave Chappelle does the same by playing his character Clayton Bigsby—a blind white supremacist who doesn't realize that he is black. It is easy to see the humour in this, since we know that Dave Chappelle isn't actually blind, or a white supremacist. That's why it's funny.

Racial Humor Helps All of Us Get the Joke

But what happens when the audience can't quite tell which racist remark is, in fact, a parody? In the case of Borat/Cohen, it is obvious when Borat is Borat, and Cohen is Cohen. Even one of Borat's detractors, the Anti-Defamation League, recognized how the country-western incident worked to expose common anti-Semitic sentiment. (But it still wasn't amused.)

But in Sarah Silverman's case, it isn't so easy. Silverman is an American comic whose stand-up character is a self-obsessed "Jewish-American Princess," seen most recently in her feature-length film *Jesus Is Magic*. Her act is charged with outrageous racist statements, delivered in a convincingly serious way. She plays the naive and harmless Jewish girl whose wide-eyed innocence rules out any inappropriate behaviour or beliefs. Or does it?

During an appearance on NBC's *Late Night with Conan O'Brien* in 2002, Silverman recounted how a friend had advised her to avoid jury duty by writing a racial slur on the selection form—"something really inappropriate, like 'I hate Chinks.'" Instead, sugary-sweet Silverman explained how she wrote "I love Chinks" because she didn't want to be considered a racist. An Asian-American media watchdog group protested the use of the slur until the network apologized. Silverman did not.

Being Taboo Is Exciting

So does she really think it is OK to say Chink? Silverman never breaks character by smiling at her own outrageousness (as in, "Oh my, did I just say that aloud?"), so we're left wondering who the real Silverman is. Unlike Cohen, her act intentionally cultivates this ambivalence. If we knew, we could decide if her act is full of racist jokes or full of jokes about racism. Couldn't we?

She further satirizes the NBC incident in *Jesus Is Magic*. Playing indignant about being singled out as a racist, she discusses what happened when she was about to go onstage: "The [NBC] segment producer came over to me and said, 'Instead of nigger, say the N-word,' and I said, 'What do you want me to say for Chink?' And he said, 'Say Chink.'"

But Silverman also gets laughs with every repeat of the slur. The thrill of a taboo word delights. Comedian Dave Chappelle knows this, too, and endlessly used the slur "nigger" on his sketch series *The Chappelle Show*. But when it became obvious that loyal viewers, many of them white, were laughing a bit too hard when he said it (and perhaps no longer found the word a problem), Chappelle wondered what his comedy was reinforcing. He walked out of a U.S. $50-million contract with Comedy Central, citing creative differences with the network as [the] reason for quitting.

Exploitation or Satirization

If slurs sell, are Silverman and Cohen truly subverting racism through race parody, or are they exploiting racist stereotypes to make a buck? The answer lies partially in the comedian's relationship to the audience and what experience they share. It's all about context. In the stand-up act of Indo-Canadian comic Russell Peters, he establishes this by asking who's Chinese, Jamaican, Taiwanese, etc., before he goes on to satirize these groups in relation to his Indian parents, friends and himself. So it's one thing when an Indian uses a self-naming slur; but it's another when a white comedian uses the same slur, over and over, continuing a long and systemic history of racial prejudice.

The character of Borat illustrates this question of context as well. While at first he seems to be parodying the "backward" and culturally inappropriate foreigner, in the end, it is his prodding of everyday Americans into expressing their equally racist assumptions that provides comedic effect.

Sandy Huffaker and PoliticalCartoons.com.

Race-Based Humor Challenges Us in a Good Way

Not everyone Borat talks to is exposed as a racist. Some ignore or politely refute his virulently anti-Semitic and misogynist claims. Their discomfort is palpable, and the audience feels uneasy too. For how would we respond to Borat if we met him on the street? How does this satire challenge our complacency toward racism, anti-Semitism and sexism?

Both Silverman's and Cohen's comedy suggest they are also satirizing us, the audience—if we laugh at the ignorance of these characters, we distance ourselves from their racism, because that's not us. We can laugh with impunity in the dark theatre, feeling superior. Or we can walk out, feeling anger about the exploitation (often by white comedians) of our painful experiences of systemic oppression. Comedy doesn't ever have to say outright, "This is a problem. Let's do something about it."

Charting a Course Using Racial Humor

Silverman has her own surprisingly cogent answer to the central dilemma of the racist joke. "We refrain from making fun of people that scare us," she quips. This is likely why Silverman's producer thought it acceptable to use a slur against Asians (stereotypically portrayed as docile and servile), but not blacks (stereotypically portrayed as violent). It is also why Cohen, as Borat, can misrepresent little-known Kazakh culture to comedic effect without any particular repercussions from that country. The power to joke is just that: power.

We can't expect the comedian to do all the work—the audience also must work to "get" the joke—not just by seeing its humour, but recognizing our personal stake in the comedy. Our reactions to race humour form a map of our comforts, anxieties, fears and responsibilities about race. We would do well to chart a course by it.

SIXTEEN

Affirmative Action Helps Overcome Discrimination

Eric Stoller

In the following selection blogger Eric Stoller explains why he believes affirmative action is a necessary part of school admissions and employment hiring practices. He argues that America continues to be racially biased, and thus affirmative action helps open doors for people who have otherwise been denied such opportunities. Furthermore, Stoller argues, increasing diversity creates better environments in workplaces and schools because they are filled with people who bring valuably different skills and experiences to the table. Stoller concludes that affirmative action helps end discrimination and creates new opportunities for people who have led disadvantaged lives.

Stoller is the founder of ericstoller.com, a blog that offers opinions on a variety of topics, including education, social justice, and technology.

Six years ago while I was nearing graduation for my undergraduate degree I was asked the following question, "Aren't you afraid that you won't be able to get a job?" I was not immediately certain as to the context of the question, but upon further inquiry, I soon found that the questioner was worried I would not be hired for jobs because I was white (and a man). This was the

Eric Stoller, "Affirmative Action," *Ericstoller.com*, March 4, 2004. Reproduced by permission.

first time I had really thought about what affirmative action was, and what it might mean to me. My thoughts regarding affirmative action had mainly been influenced by my family and the media. For the most part, I thought that affirmative action was a good thing, but I did not know why I thought that way. Doubts about affirmative action being a positive policy seeped into my head while I was conducting my first job search. I believed that reverse-racism and/or reverse-discrimination existed and that I would have to "watch my back."

Female construction employees work at a federal building site. Affirmative action programs are intended to give women access to opportunities traditionally dominated by men, and minorities access to opportunities dominated by whites.

The Myth That Hard Work Is All It Takes

Today, I have read, thought, and conversed about affirmative action. I feel that I used to believe in the myth of meritocracy. "Everyone can succeed as long as they work hard," floated around inside my head and veiled my mind from the truth. I believe that the United States is not a meritocracy and that affirmative action is extremely necessary. Why is it necessary? Because the United States is a system built upon the backbreaking labor, systematic abuse, and marginalization of people of color, women, and other subordinate groups. Affirmative action is a program that seeks to provide equity for these marginalized groups. It helps to create a balance against the white supremacist patriarchy in which we live.

Several arguments exist which seek to discredit or devalue affirmative action. Two arguments that I hear frequently include: 1) Affirmative action gives jobs to people of color who are not qualified and they only receive said job due to this program. 2) White men are discriminated against because of the inherent reverse-racism within affirmative action programs.

Affirmative Action Helps Qualified People Get Jobs

The first argument seems to stem from the belief that the definitions of what makes for a "qualified" employee are usually in the hands of white folks. Most of the institutions in the United States are chaired, governed, and otherwise presided over by white people. When a person of color is hired for a job, how often is their competency called into question? Let's consider the following scenario: A white person interviews and is consequently hired for a job. I would posit that no one says to themselves, "wow, they must have been hired because they are white." It does not happen. However, if a person of color goes through the same process there will be doubters. I think that a lot of people will say quite negatively, "Yep, here's another example of affirmative action hiring a person of color. I hope they can do the job." The white person is given an air of competency simply because of their whiteness. Affirmative action opens up spaces for marginalized individuals to combat the inequalities of white supremacy within the realm of employment.

Affirmative Action Can Help the Disadvantaged

Minorities continue to have the highest unemployment and poverty rates in the United States. Many believe that affirmative action policies can help correct these inequities.

Unemployment Rate

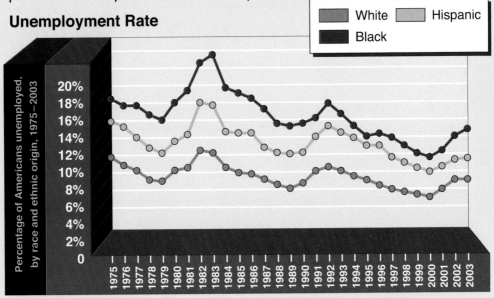

Source: Labor Force Statistics from the Current Population Survey, May 2004, U.S. Bureau of Labor Statistics.

Poverty Rate

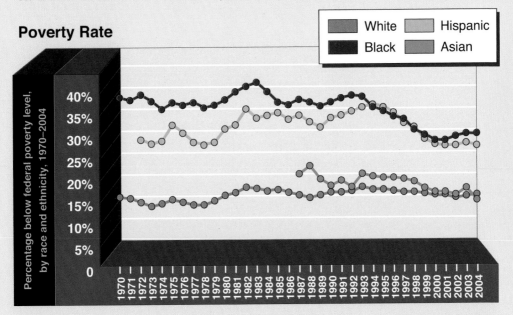

Source: "Income, Poverty and Health Insurance Coverage in the United States: 2004," August 2006, U.S. Census Bureau.

The second argument against affirmative action is constructed within a context that is void of a historical context and knowledge of the existence of institutionalized racism. Historically speaking, white men have been in positions of power over everyone. This "power over" has saturated the United States for over one hundred years. White privilege exists because of racist tactics, strategies, and actions of the dominant paradigm. The dominant paradigm is hierarchical and white men sit atop this ladder. To say that white men are discriminated against during hiring processes due to affirmative action is like saying white men are not in power. It is a falsity that is used to erode affirmative action and to maintain the ladder of white supremacist power. I believe that racism is something that white people perpetuate.

Helping to Overcome Institutionalized Racism

Racism is institutionalized and spread into white consciousness like a virus. White men can be discriminated against, because discrimination is different from racism. It is true that I might be discriminated against in my lifetime, but not by affirmative action programs. Affirmative action programs will take a look at my qualifications and the qualifications of a person of color, a woman, etc. and if our qualifications are the same then I will not get the job. For racism to end, white people have to be willing to give up their unearned privileges and power. The same principle applies to sexism, heterosexism, ableism, and lookism. I feel that it is part of my anti-racist philosophy to rejoice in the fact that I did not get a job because of the mere fact that I am white. There are plenty of jobs that I can get.

So, rejoice in the knowledge that affirmative action exists. Affirmative action helps to restore the dignity of people in oppressed groups as well as people in oppressor groups. Affirmative action places all those who seek to work for the government at the starting gate of employment processes, instead of allowing the dominant paradigm to start ahead of those who have been, and currently are, marginalized.

SEVENTEEN

Affirmative Action Does Not Help Overcome Discrimination

Marie Gryphon

In the following selection Marie Gryphon argues that affirmative action should be dismantled because it does not help overcome discrimination. She claims that affirmative action does not send additional minority students to college and cites statistics that show as many blacks enroll in college today as before affirmative action policies were adopted. Gryphon argues that the reason many minorities do not earn college degrees is not because they fail to be admitted to universities but because they fail to finish high school with college-appropriate credentials. Gryphon also presents evidence showing that affirmative action policies actually hurt those they are intended to help by placing them in competitive environments they are not adequately prepared for. For these reasons, Gryphon concludes that affirmative action is a liberal myth that should be abandoned in the pursuit to overcome discrimination.

Gryphon is a lawyer and policy analyst with the Cato Institute's Center for Educational Freedom, the publisher of this viewpoint.

Marie Gryphon, "The Affirmative Action Myth," Cato Institute Policy Analysis, vol. 540, April 13, 2005, pp. 1, 2-7, 17. Copyright © 2005 Cato Institute. All rights reserved. Reproduced by permission.

In the wake of the Supreme Court's recent [2005] decision to uphold university admissions preferences, affirmative action remains a deeply divisive issue. But recent research shows that college admissions preferences do not offer even the practical benefits claimed by their supporters. Because preferences do not help minority students, policymakers and administrators of all political persuasions should oppose their use.

The Affirmative Action Myth

Affirmative action defenders frequently and correctly tout the importance of college to the goal of improving life prospects. But preferences at selective schools have not increased college access. They cannot do so because most minority students leave high school without the minimum qualifications to attend any four-year school. Only outreach and better high school preparation can reduce overall racial disparities in American colleges.

Nor do preferences increase the wages of students who attend more selective schools as a result of affirmative action. When equally prepared students are compared, recent research shows that those who attend less selective institutions make just as much money as do their counterparts from more selective schools.

No Concrete Benefits

Affirmative action produces no concrete benefits to minority groups, but it does produce several significant harms. First, a phenomenon called the "ratchet effect" means that preferences at a handful of top schools, including state flagship institutions, can worsen racial disparities in academic preparation at all other American colleges and universities, including those that do not use admissions preferences. This effect results in painfully large gaps in academic preparation between minority students and others on campuses around the country.

Recent sociological research demonstrates that preferences hurt campus race relationships. Worse, they harm minority student performance by activating fears of confirming negative group stereotypes, lowering grades, and reducing college completion rates among preferred students.

Research shows that skills, not credentials, can narrow socio-economic gaps between white and minority families. Policymakers should end the harmful practice of racial preferences in college admissions. Instead, they should work to close the critical skills gap by implementing school choice reforms and setting higher academic expectations for students of all backgrounds. . . .

Preferences Do Not Send More Minority Students to College

Affirmative action defenders frequently and correctly tout the importance of college to the goal of improving life prospects.

Ward Connerly speaks to a crowd at Kalamazoo College in Kalamazoo, Michigan. As chairman of the American Civil Rights Coalition, Connerly led a successful effort to outlaw affirmative action in the state, reflecting his view that it is a discriminatory and counterproductive practice.

[Researchers] Bowen and Bok comment at length about the importance of a college education. They write, "The growing numbers of blacks graduating from colleges and professional schools, and the consequent increase in black managers and professionals, have led to the gradual emergence of a larger black middle class." They are right. Few things foster professional success more reliably than a college education. College has helped many minority students achieve middle-class lives.

NAACP attorney William Taylor's remarks are typical of efforts to connect racial preferences at elite schools to the issue of college access: "There can also be little question that affirmative action policies of colleges and universities [have] played a large role in the major increases in minority college enrollment that we saw during the 1970s and 1980s." But preferences have not increased college access. In fact, Thomas Sowell observes that black college enrollment increased at least as quickly in the 1950s and early 1960s, prior to the establishment of affirmative action policies, as it did afterwards.

The reason that affirmative action does not affect college access is that most four-year colleges and universities in America are not selective; they take anyone with a standard high school education. Preferences are policy only at the 20–30 percent of American colleges that have substantially more applicants than places. Students attending those schools have many other college options.

The Problem Is Not Admission

The reason that minority students do not get college degrees as often as white students is not competitive admissions policies. Rather, the problem is that most minority students leave high school without the minimum credentials necessary to attend any four-year school, selective or not.

Freshmen must be "college ready" at almost all four-year colleges. That means that students must be literate, have a high school diploma, and have taken certain minimum coursework. Overwhelmingly, minority students are not college ready. Political scientist Jay Greene of the Manhattan Institute found that only 20 percent of black students and 16 percent of Hispanic students leave high school with these basic requirements.

Minority underrepresentation in college is caused by public schools' failure to prepare minority students. It is a failure that affirmative action does not remedy. "College-ready" minorities are already slightly more likely to attend college than their white counterparts. Even if affirmative action were ended, every minority student affected by the policy change would have a college opportunity at some four-year school. . . .

Preferences Do Not Increase Earning Power

No contention is more central to The Myth [that affirmative action is necessary] than that preferences are a catalyst for upward financial mobility. Moderate supporters of affirmative action tolerate the social costs of preferences because they hope that preferences will improve the concrete well-being of minority students after graduation.

Indeed, research used to suggest that attending a more selective college was related to substantial, though not huge, financial gains. Generally, studies indicated that attending a school with an average SAT score 100 points higher would increase a student's future earnings by 3–7 percent.

But those studies suffered from a serious methodological problem. They were unable to take into account many of the factors that colleges look at when deciding which students to admit. Academic researchers generally have only high school GPA and SAT scores at their disposal, so they must compare students with the same grades and scores and assume that the students are otherwise the same. Teacher recommendations, the difficulty of the high school attended, and student motivation as reflected in an admissions essay are unavailable to researchers. As a result, researchers attributed wage premiums to "equally qualified" students who attended more prestigious schools, when in fact the students were not equally qualified at all.

But recent research has shown that this part of The Myth, like the others, is untrue. Attendance at a more selective school does not raise students' future incomes, regardless of race.

Going to a School That Uses Preferences Is Not Important

Economists Stacy Dale and Alan Krueger developed an ingenious method to solve these problems and compare students who were truly alike. They "matched" several thousand students nationwide on the basis of selectivity of the schools that accepted and rejected them and compared members of the matched groups only to each other. This was possible because only 62 percent of students in the sample chose to attend the most selective school that accepted them.

Thus, Dale and Krueger were able to compare students who were accepted by a top tier school and actually attended that school to students who were accepted to that same top school but chose instead to attend a less selective school. Comparing students with identical acceptances takes into account (and "controls for") all of the factors that colleges take into account when they accept students.

Dale and Krueger found that when genuinely equivalent students were compared, students attending less selective schools *made just as much money as* students who attended more selective schools. The idea that a selective university will make you rich is just another part of The Myth.

Affirmative Action Is Not Popular

Affirmative action supporters frequently claim popular support for their cause among elite college students, graduates, and faculty. Bowen and Bok, for example, find that admissions preferences are popular on the basis of surveys showing that college alums thought their institutions ought to place even more emphasis on diversity.

But they got the "right" answer by asking the wrong question. Students and faculty do value diversity, but that does not mean that they support differential admissions standards in order to achieve racial balance. Most polls suggest that students and faculty are closely divided on the issue of preferences but that majorities of both groups do not support them.

A poll of Berkeley students taken at the time that Proposition 209, which banned preferences in state university admissions, was on the ballot in California showed that most students opposed

American Attitudes About Affirmative Action

The majority of people, black and white, say they support programs that give "assistance" to minorities, but the majority of whites oppose giving minorities "preference."

Do you support or oppose government and private programs that give women, blacks, and other minorities assistance – but not preference – getting into college, getting a job, or getting a promotion?

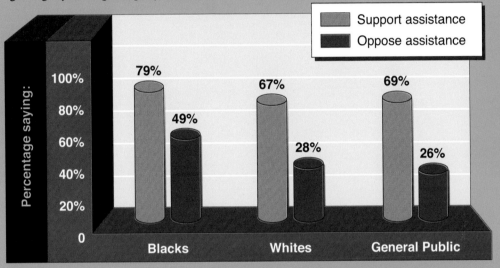

Do you support or oppose government and private programs that give women, blacks, and other minorities preference getting into college, getting a job, or getting a promotion?

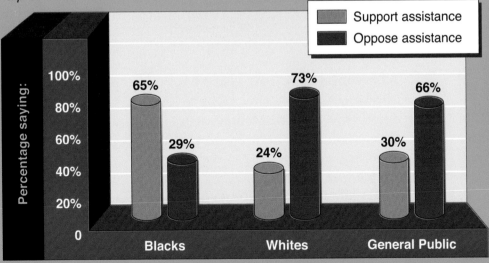

Source: ABC News / Washington Post, January 2003.

affirmative action. *New York Times* columnist James Traub reported, "Berkeley students, it turns out, are like most Americans: they want diversity without the zero-sum calculus that inevitably accompanies affirmative action." Similarly, a Roper poll found that UC faculty members were split on the issue, with 48 percent opposing admissions preferences and only 31 percent expressing support.

Students and Faculty Oppose Racial Preferences

Aware of these polls, economists Harry Holzer and David Neumark, who support preferences, make a more cautious statement, that "public opinion polls still indicate public support for some forms of affirmative action." They are right, but only those forms of "affirmative action" that do not involve preferences (such as outreach and remediation) command support. Prof. Stephen Cole reports, "Surveys suggest that a majority of both students and faculty are opposed to policies in which race trumps qualifications."

Moreover, in highly charged university environments, faculty members are sometimes afraid to admit that they oppose preferences. Berkeley professor Martin Trow writes, "Very few academics wish to offend both the senior administrators who govern their careers and budgets and the well-organized affirmative action pressure groups that will quickly stereotype faculty members as 'racists' or, at very least, 'right-wingers.'" Thomas Sowell recalls "bitter fights" that have erupted among faculty members about whether affirmative action policies should be decided by secret ballot, because whether the votes were public might affect the results.

Affirmative Action Does More Harm than Good

The foregoing suggests that many benefits attributed to preferences do not exist. But The Myth is worse than useless. It perpetuates a policy that is harmful to students of all backgrounds, especially minority students.

That is the argument against preferences that their supporters assail most energetically. Bowen and Bok optimistically asserted that their findings "have essentially disposed of the 'harm-the-beneficiary' line of argument. There is no empirical support for it." This epitaph has proved premature. Recent research contradicts this claim on the basis of far more sophisticated methods than those used by the former university presidents.

Dropout Rates

Black students are less likely than white students to graduate from any institution of higher learning. Latino students also graduate at relatively low rates. That persistent problem depresses the wages of minority workers and is of concern to policymakers who seek to close the socioeconomic gaps between racial groups. Opponents of affirmative action have long contended that preferences increase minority dropout rates.

Bowen and Bok argued on the basis of SAT scores alone that equally qualified students are actually more likely to graduate if they attend more selective schools. However, their analysis assumes that the average minority student with an SAT score of 1250 at the University of Michigan is as academically prepared as the average minority student with the same SAT score at Yale. That is unlikely. The student accepted to Yale probably presented additional evidence, such as advanced placement work or an excellent essay, that made their application more attractive by reflecting skills likely to be useful in college. Bowen and Bok admit that SAT scores alone do not reflect differences between students as well as instruments that combine several measures of preparedness.

Moreover, like efforts to predict the effect of college selectivity on wages, predicting the effect of selectivity on dropout rates is made difficult by the presence of unobserved factors, such as motivation, that affect student outcomes. The techniques used by Bowen and Bok cannot take these differences into account.

Sociologist Robert Lerner, now commissioner of the National Center for Education Statistics, observed, "Despite its size, *The Shape of the River* includes largely cursory statistical analysis of applicant data." Bowen and Bok are aware that their work is rudimentary. "In due course," they write, "we expect others, using more sophisticated econometric techniques, to expand the analysis presented here. . . ."

Let's Abandon Affirmative Action

Affirmative action cannot solve the American dilemma of racial inequality. Preferences are designed to harness what their boosters thought would be formidable power of prestige in getting ahead. But those who hope to ride credentials into the sunset of racial equality have saddled the wrong horse. Not only do preferences fail to narrow racial disparities in income and educational attainment, they harm students of all backgrounds. Only no-fuss integration and a focus on building real skills will lead to success.

What You Should Know About Discrimination

Aseries of laws prohibit discrimination based on race, color, sex, religion, national origin, age, and disability.

Title VII of the Civil Rights Act of 1964

Title VII was landmark legislation that protects individuals against discrimination in the workplace. The legislation

- protects against employment discrimination on the basis of race, skin color, national origin, sex, or religion. The law makes it illegal to discriminate against any employee or job applicant in regard to hiring, termination, promotion, compensation, job training, or any other term, condition, or privilege of employment.

- prohibits employment decisions based on stereotypes and assumptions about abilities, traits, qualities, or performance. Title VII prohibits both intentional discrimination and neutral job policies that disproportionately exclude minorities and that are not job-related.

- prohibits the denial of equal employment opportunity because of association with an individual of a different race; membership in or association with ethnic-based organizations or groups; or attendance or participation in schools or places of worship generally associated with certain minority groups.

- prohibits discrimination on the basis of a condition which largely affects one race. For example, sickle cell anemia predominantly occurs in African Americans. Policies that exclude individuals with sickle cell anemia are only legal if they are job-related and constitute a business necessity.

- prohibits harassment on the basis of race and color. Ethnic slurs, racial "jokes," offensive or derogatory comments, or other verbal or physical conduct based on an individual's race/color constitutes unlawful harassment, especially if the conduct creates an intimidating, hostile, or offensive working environment, or interferes with the individual's work performance.

- prohibits segregation and classification of employees. It also prohibits assigning primarily minorities to predominantly minority establishments or geographic areas. Under Title VII it is also illegal to exclude minorities from certain positions.

- prohibits employers from discriminating against individuals because of their religion. The Act also requires employers to, within reason, accommodate the religious practices of an employee.

Equal Pay Act of 1963
Passed in 1963 the Equal Pay Act requires that men and women be given equal pay for equal work in the same establishment:

- Employers may not pay unequal wages to men and women who perform jobs that require substantially equal skill, effort, and responsibility, and that are performed under similar working conditions within the same establishment.

- Pay differentials are permitted when they are based on seniority, merit, quantity or quality of production, or a factor other than sex.

Civil Rights Act of 1968
The Civil Rights Act of 1968 prohibits the following forms of discrimination:

- refusal to sell or rent property on the basis of race, color, religion, or national origin (those with disabilities and families with children were added to the list of protected classes by the Fair Housing Amendments Act of 1988).

- discrimination against a person in the terms, conditions, or privilege of the sale or rental of a dwelling.

- advertising the sale or rental of property indicating preference of discrimination based on race, color, religion, or national origin (including people with disabilities and families with children as of 1988).

- coercing, threatening, intimidating, or interfering with a person's housing rights based on discriminatory reasons.

Age Discrimination in Employment Act of 1967

- prohibits employment discrimination nationwide based on age with respect to employees forty years of age or older.

- addresses the difficulty older workers face in obtaining new employment after being displaced from their jobs.

Sections 501 of the Rehabilitation Act of 1973

- prohibits employment discrimination against individuals with disabilities in the federal sector.

Titles I and V of the Americans with Disabilities Act of 1990

- prohibits private employers, state and local governments, employment agencies and labor unions from discriminating against qualified individuals with disabilities in job application procedures, hiring, firing, advancement, compensation, job training, and other terms, conditions, and privileges of employment.

- covers employers with fifteen or more employees, including state and local governments.

- applies to employment agencies, labor organizations, and federal sector employees under Section 501.

- defines an individual with a disability as a person who:
  - has a physical or mental impairment that substantially limits one or more major life activities;
  - has a record of such an impairment; or
  - is regarded as having such an impairment.
- requires employers to reasonably accommodate employees with disabilities, including
  - making existing facilities used by employees readily accessible to and usable by persons with disabilities;
  - job restructuring, modifying work schedules, reassignment to a vacant position;
  - acquiring or modifying equipment or devices, adjusting or modifying examinations, training materials, or policies, and providing qualified readers or interpreters.
- protects employers from lowering quality or production standards to make an accommodation; protects employers from being obligated to provide personal items such as glasses or hearing aids.
- prohibits employers from asking job applicants about the existence, nature, or severity of a disability. Applicants may be asked about their ability to perform specific job functions. A job offer may be conditioned on the results of a medical examination, but only if the examination is required for all entering employees in similar jobs. Medical examinations of employees must be job-related and consistent with the employer's business needs.

Civil Rights Act of 1991

- strengthens existing civil rights laws and provides for damages in the event of intentional employment discrimination.

What You Should Do About Discrimination

Discrimination is a divisive issue that generates heated debate. It touches on subjects relating to race, ethnicity, religion, sexual orientation, gender, and age. It involves disputing what constitutes discrimination and identifying whether or not discrimination against particular groups continues to be a serious problem. Both sides in the debate insist their perspectives are correct and the course of action they advocate is prudent. But it is not possible for everyone to be correct all of the time. With so many well-argued positions, how can you decide whom to agree with? How can you develop an informed opinion on this issue? How should you present well-made arguments to persuade others that your point of view is correct? Finally, what can you do to reduce the occurrence of discrimination in your family, school, or community?

Evaluate Your Sources of Information

In forming your opinion on any topic it is important to evaluate the sources of the information you have gathered. The authors of books, magazine articles, newspaper editorials, government reports, and other documents generally have a point of view, and even if they are not frankly trying to enlist the reader's support, their personal interests or biases may be reflected in their writing. To help you separate fact from opinion and judge the merit of a writer's argument, consider the writer's credentials and the nature and purposes of the organizations he or she is associated with.

For example, if you read a report published by the Council on American-Islamic Relations (CAIR), an organization whose mission is to protect the civil liberties of American Muslims, you should expect the author to present information that emphasizes instances of discrimination against Muslims and omit or discount criticisms from opponents that discrimination against Muslims is not on the rise. On the other hand, a report published by the Department of

Homeland Security, the governmental organization charged with protecting Americans against terrorism, is likely to produce evidence that argues American Muslims are not racially profiled and will downplay or discount arguments that claim American Muslims are unfairly targeted by authorities.

While the information in both of these documents may be entirely valid, each author is likely to stress the facts that support his or her views as well as those of whatever organization he or she represents. In short, rather than simply accepting all information at face value, read critically and be aware of the biases that influence your sources.

Define the Debate

In addition to evaluating your sources, you must learn to articulate where you stand on issues relating to discrimination. This involves defining the debate surrounding particular topics. Only after you understand what is at the heart of the debate can you decide for yourself whether you think certain practices are in fact discriminatory or not. For example, there is much debate over whether prohibiting gay marriage counts as discrimination. To some, for example, it is discriminatory to deny gay couples the same right to marry that straight couples enjoy. They liken the right to marry to the right to vote that was denied blacks and women in the early twentieth century and view the fight to legalize gay marriage as the next logical step in the fight for civil rights. On the other hand, those who do not believe banning gay marriage counts as discrimination argue that something can only be discriminatory if the identical right is not extended to one party. Using that definition, they argue that gay people do in fact have the same right to marry that straight people have—they too can get married as the definition of marriage now stands, which is a union between a man and a woman. So gay people can marry, provided they are willing to marry someone of the opposite sex. Defining the debate on whether banning gay marriage counts as discrimination or not, in other words, involves clarifying what discrimination is and what gay people are actually being denied. It will be necessary to define this and other issues presented in this book before you are able to adequately analyze them. Take some time to think about what you know about the gay marriage debate. Do you consider it to be an issue of discrimination? Why or why not?

Examine Your Values

Discrimination is often a result of what is learned in a person's environment. Sometimes people hold discriminatory beliefs because as a child they heard their parents or grandparents make derogatory comments; others may have grown up in an era where discrimination against women or minorities was more common, and thus accepted. Take some time to explore your thoughts on this issue. Look inside yourself and be honest about any discriminatory thoughts, tendencies, or preferences you may hold. Recognize that your personal experience may color your opinion and values on the issue. Perhaps you or someone you love has been victimized in a way that left a mark, causing you to make a judgment about an entire group. Perhaps you have allowed yourself to believe certain things about a group of people without even knowing anyone of that group personally. If you have such beliefs, explore why you hold them, and challenge yourself to think in new terms. Commit to appreciating every person as an individual rather than as part of a group.

It is also helpful to articulate your values when considering the effects of potentially discriminatory practices, such as the use of ethnic mascots or race-based humor. To some, race-based humor is an excellent way to fight racism and discrimination by showing how ridiculous people who hold discriminatory beliefs appear out of context. To others, race-based humor is callous, insensitive, and a cheap, exploitative way to get a laugh. Carefully consider some of the race-based humor you have been exposed to. What do you think? Do such comedy routines relieve or reinforce stereotypes and discrimination?

Effect Change in Your Community

Once you decide where you stand on issues pertaining to discrimination, speak up and act out! If you see discrimination underway somewhere in your family, school, or community, work tirelessly to teach people to think outside the box. Challenge others to be honest about their prejudices. Ask them why they formed prejudices in the first place, and encourage them to think beyond stereotypes. Conversely, if you know someone, or if you yourself have been the victim of discrimination, take steps to understand why the situation occurred and work to forgive the person who discriminated against you. Avoid falling into the trap of practicing reverse discrimination—that is, making stereotypes about a group of people because someone of that group did the same to you.

If you want to get involved in broader issues pertaining to discrimination—for example, to protest a team mascot you feel is discriminatory or to oppose gay marriage on the grounds that it is not discriminatory—use channels in your community to make your voice heard. Write a well-researched article for your school paper or a letter to the editor of a community news magazine or journal. Start a blog and voice your thoughts on the Internet. Participate in fund-raising efforts for causes that promote a position you feel strongly in favor of.

Regardless of whether you take action—and what type of action you take—once you have thoroughly researched the topic and examined your own values, you will be able to participate intelligently in debates related to discrimination. Your critical thinking skills will be sharper the next time you are called on to think about a controversial issue and decide where you stand.

ORGANIZATIONS TO CONTACT

The editors have compiled the following list of organizations concerned with the issues debated in this book. The descriptions are derived from materials provided by the organizations. All have publications or information available for interested readers. The list was compiled on the date of publication of the present volume; the information provided here may change. Be aware that many organizations take several weeks or longer to respond to inquiries, so allow as much time as possible.

Adversity.Net
PO Box 7099, Silver Spring, MD 20907-7099
(301) 588-0778
e-mail: editor@adversity.net
Web site: www.adversity.net

Adversity.Net opposes racial discrimination against anyone, including racial discrimination against nonminorities. It publishes fact sheets and case histories regarding reverse discrimination.

American-Arab Anti-Discrimination Committee (ADC)
4201 Connecticut Ave. NW, Suite 300, Washington, DC 20008
(202) 244-2990
e-mail: ADC@adc.org
Web site: www.adc.org

This organization fights anti-Arab stereotyping in the media and works to protect Arab-Americans from discrimination and hate crimes. It publishes a bimonthly newsletter, the *Chronicle*; issue papers and special reports; community studies; legal, media, and educational guides; and action alerts.

American Civil Liberties Union (ACLU)
125 Broad St., 18th Floor, New York, NY 10004
(212) 549-2500
Web site: www.aclu.org

The ACLU is a national organization that works to defend Americans' civil rights as guaranteed by the U.S. Constitution. The ACLU publishes and distributes policy statements, pamphlets, and the semiannual newsletter *Civil Liberties Alert*.

American Immigration Control Foundation (AICF)
PO Box 525, Monterey, VA 24465
(703) 468-2022

The AICF is a research and educational organization whose primary goal is to promote a reasonable immigration policy based on national interests and needs. The foundation educates the public on what its members believe are the disastrous effects of uncontrolled immigration.

Amnesty International (AI)
322 Eighth Ave., New York, NY 10004-2400
(212) 807-8400
(800) AMNESTY (266-3789)
Web site: www.amnesty-usa.org.

Founded in 1961, AI is a grassroots activist organization that aims to free all nonviolent people who have been imprisoned because of their beliefs, ethnic origin, sex, color, or language. The *Amnesty International Report* is published annually, and other reports are available online and by mail.

Cato Institute
1000 Massachusetts Ave. NW, Washington, DC 20001-5403
(202) 842-0200
e-mail: cato@cato.org
Web site: www.cato.org

The Cato Institute is a libertarian public policy research foundation dedicated to limiting the role of government and protecting individual liberties. It researches claims of discrimination and opposes affirmative action. The institute offers numerous publications, including the *Cato Journal*, the bimonthly newsletter *Cato Policy Report*, and the quarterly magazine *Regulation*.

Center for the Study of Popular Culture (CSPC)
9911 W. Pico Blvd., Suite 1290, Los Angeles, CA 90035
(310) 843-3699
Web site: www.cspc.org

CSPC is a conservative educational organization that addresses topics such as political correctness, cultural diversity, and discrimination. Its civil rights project promotes equal opportunity for all individuals and provides legal assistance to citizens challenging affirmative action. The center publishes four magazines: *Heterodoxy*, *Defender*, *Report Card*, and *COMINT*.

Citizens' Commission on Civil Rights (CCCR)
2000 M St. NW, Suite 400, Washington, DC 20036
(202) 659-5565
e-mail: citizens@cccr.org
Web site: www.cccr.org

CCCR monitors the federal government's enforcement of antidiscrimination laws and promotes equal opportunity for all. It publishes reports on affirmative action and desegregation as well as the book *One Nation Indivisible: The Civil Rights Challenge for the 1990s*.

Commission for Racial Justice (CRJ)
700 Prospect Ave., Cleveland, OH 44115-1110
(216) 736-2100

CRJ was formed in 1963 by the United Church of Christ in response to racial tensions gripping the nation at that time. Its goal is a peaceful, dignified society where all men and women are equal. CRJ publishes various documents and books, such as *Racism and the Pursuit of Racial Justice* and *A National Symposium on Race and Housing in the United States: Challenges for the 21st Century*.

Council on American-Islamic Relations (CAIR)
453 New Jersey Avenue SE, Washington, DC 20003
(202) 488-8787
e-mail: cair@cair-net.org
Web site: www.cair-net.org

CAIR is a nonprofit membership organization that presents an Islamic perspective to public policy issues and challenges the misrepresentation of Islam and Muslims. It fights discrimination against Muslims in America and lobbies political leaders on issues related to Islam. Its publications include the quarterly newsletter *CAIR News*, reports on Muslim civil rights issues, and periodic action alerts.

Equal Rights Marriage Fund (ERMF)
2001 M St. NW, Washington, DC 20036
(202) 822-6546

The ERMF is dedicated to the legalization of gay and lesbian marriage and serves as a national clearinghouse for information on same-sex marriage. The organization publishes several brochures and articles, including *Gay Marriage: A Civil Right*.

Families and Work Institute
330 Seventh Ave., New York, NY 10001
(212) 465-2044
Web site: www.familiesandwork.org

The institute is a research and planning organization that develops new approaches to balancing the continuing need for workplace productivity with the changing needs of American families. More than forty research reports are available for sale from the institute, including *The Changing Workforce: Highlights of the National Study*, *Women: The New Providers*, *Community Mobilization: Strategies to Support Young Children and Their Families*, and *An Examination of the Impact of Family-Friendly Policies on the Glass Ceiling*.

Family Research Council (FRC)
700 13th St. NW, Suite 500, Washington, DC 20005
(202) 393-2100

The council is a research, resource, and educational organization that promotes the traditional family, which the council defines as a group of people bound by marriage, blood, or adoption. The council opposes gay marriage and adoption rights. It publishes numerous reports from a conservative perspective on issues affecting the family, including homosexuality. These publications include the monthly newsletter *Washington Watch* and bimonthly journal *Family Policy*.

Family Research Institute (FRI)

PO Box 62640, Colorado Springs, CO 80962-0640
(303) 681-3113
Web site: www.familyresearchinst.org

The FRI distributes information about family, sexuality, and substance abuse issues. It believes that strengthening marriage would reduce many social problems, including crime, poverty, and sexually transmitted diseases. The institute publishes the bimonthly newsletter *Family Research Report* as well as the position paper "What's Wrong with Gay Marriage?"

Focus on the Family

8605 Explorer Dr., Colorado Springs, CO 80920
(800) 232-6459
Web site: www.family.org

Focus on the Family is a conservative Christian organization that promotes traditional family values and gender roles. Its publications include the monthly magazine *Focus on the Family* and the reports "Setting the Record Straight: What Research Really Says About the Social Consequences of Homosexuality," "No-Fault Fallout: The Grim Aftermath of Modern Divorce Law and How to Change It," "Only a Piece of Paper? The Unquestionable Benefits of Lifelong Marriage," and "'Only a Piece of Paper?' The Social Significance of the Marriage License and the Negative Consequences of Cohabitation."

Heritage Foundation

214 Massachusetts Ave. NE, Washington, DC 20002-4999
(202) 546-4400
e-mail: info@heritage.org
Web site: www.heritage.org

The foundation is a conservative public policy research institute that advocates free-market principles, individual liberty, and limited government. It believes the private sector, not government, should be relied upon to ease social problems and to improve the status of minorities.

Hispanic Policy Development Project (HPDP)

1001 Connecticut Ave. NW, Suite 901, Washington, DC 20036
(202) 822-8414

HPDP encourages the analysis of public policies affecting Hispanics in the United States, particularly the education, training, and employment of Hispanic youth. It publishes a number of books and pamphlets, including *Together Is Better: Building Strong Partnerships Between Schools and Hispanic Parents*.

Howard Center for Family, Religion, and Society
934 North Main St., Rockford, IL 61103
(815) 964-5819
Web site: http://profam.org/Default.htm

The purpose of the Howard Center is to provide research and understanding that demonstrates and affirms family and religion as the foundation of a virtuous and free society. The center believes that the natural family is the fundamental unit of society. The primary mission of the Howard Center is to provide a clearinghouse of useful and relevant information to support families and their defenders throughout the world. The center publishes the monthly journal *Family in America* and the *Religion and Society Report*.

Islamic Supreme Council of America (ISCA)
1400 Sixteenth St. NW, Room B112, Washington, DC 20036
(202) 939-3400
e-mail: staff@islamicsupremecouncil.org
Web site: www.islamicsupremecouncil.org

The ISCA is a nongovernmental religious organization that promotes Islam in America both by providing practical solutions to American Muslims in integrating Islamic teachings with American culture and by teaching non-Muslims that Islam is a religion of moderation, peace, and tolerance. It strongly condemns Islamic extremists and all forms of terrorism. Its Web site includes statements, commentaries, and reports on terrorism, including *Usama bin Laden: A Legend Gone Wrong* and *Jihad: A Misunderstood Concept from Islam*.

National Association for the Advancement of Colored People (NAACP)
4805 Mt. Hope Dr., Baltimore, MD 21215-3297
(410) 358-8900

The NAACP is the oldest and largest civil rights organization in the United States. Its principal objective is to ensure the political, educational, social, and economic equality of minorities. It publishes the magazine *Crisis* ten times a year as well as a variety of newsletters, books, and pamphlets.

National Committee on Pay Equity (NCPE)
555 New Jersey Ave. NW, Washington, DC 20001-2029
(703) 920-2010
e-mail: fairpay@pay-equity.org
Web site: www.pay-equity.org

NCPE is a national coalition of labor, women's, and civil rights organizations and individuals working to achieve pay equity by eliminating sex- and race-based wage discrimination. Its publications include the quarterly newsletter *Newsnotes* and numerous books and briefing papers on the issue of pay equity.

National Network for Immigrant and Refugee Rights (NNIRR)
310 Eighth St., Suite 307, Oakland, CA 94607
(510) 465-1984
e-mail: nnir@igc.apc.org.
Web site: www.nnir.org

The network includes community, church, labor, and legal groups committed to the cause of equal rights for all immigrants. These groups work to end discrimination and unfair treatment of illegal immigrants and refugees. It publishes the monthly newsletter *Network News*.

National Urban League
120 Wall St., 8th Floor, New York, NY 10005
(212) 558-5300
Web site: www.nul.org

A community service agency, the National Urban League aims to eliminate institutional racism in the United States. It also provides services for minorities who experience discrimination in employment, housing, welfare, and other areas. It publishes the report *The Price: A Study of the Costs of Racism in America* and the annual *State of Black America*.

Poverty and Race Research Action Council (PRRAC)
3000 Connecticut Ave. NW, Suite 200, Washington, DC 20008
(202) 387-9887
e-mail: info@prrac.org

The Poverty and Race Research Action Council is a nonpartisan, national, not-for-profit organization convened by major civil rights, civil liberties, and antipoverty groups. PRRAC's purpose is to link social science research to advocacy work in order to successfully address problems at the intersection of race and poverty. Its bimonthly publication *Poverty and Race* often includes articles on race- and income-based inequities in the United States.

The Prejudice Institute
Stephens Hall Annex, TSU, Towson, MD 21204-7097
(410) 830-2435

The Prejudice Institute is a national research center concerned with violence and intimidation motivated by prejudice. It conducts research, supplies information on model programs and legislation, and provides education and training to combat prejudicial violence. The Prejudice Institute publishes research reports, bibliographies, and the quarterly newsletter *Forum*.

United States Commission on Civil Rights
624 Ninth St. NW, Suite 500, Washington, DC 20425
(202) 376-7533

A fact-finding body, the commission reports directly to Congress and the president on the effectiveness of equal opportunity laws and programs. A catalog of its numerous publications can be obtained from its Publication Management Division.

BIBLIOGRAPHY

Books

Adalberto Aguirre Jr. and Jonathan H. Turner, *American Ethnicity: The Dynamics and Consequences of Discrimination*. New York: McGraw-Hill, 2006.

Justin Akers Chacon and Mike Davis, *No One Is Illegal: Fighting Racism and State Violence on the U.S.-Mexico Border*. Chicago: Haymarket, 2006.

Melissa Checker, *Polluted Promises: Environmental Racism and the Search for Justice in a Southern Town*. New York: New York University Press, 2005.

Joel Wm. Friedman, *Employment Discrimination Stories*. New York: Foundation, 2006.

Evan Gerstmann, *Same-Sex Marriage and the Constitution*. New York: Cambridge University Press, 2004.

Raymond F. Gregory, *Women and Workplace Discrimination: Overcoming Barriers to Gender Equality*. New Brunswick, NJ: Rutgers University Press, 2003.

J. Edward Kellough, *Understanding Affirmative Action: Politics, Discrimination, and the Search for Justice*. Washington, DC: Georgetown University Press, 2006.

Davina Kotulski, *Why You Should Give a Damn About Gay Marriage*. Los Angeles: Advocate, 2004.

Kevin Lang, *Poverty and Discrimination*. Princeton, NJ: Princeton University Press, 2007.

David Moats, *Civil Wars: A Battle for Gay Marriage*. Orlando, FL: Harcourt, 2004.

Fred L. Pincus, *Reverse Discrimination: Dismantling the Myth*. Boulder, CO: Lynne Rienner, 2003.

Jonathan Rauch, *Gay Marriage: Why It Is Good for Gays, Good for Straights, and Good for America*. New York: Times Books-Henry Holt, 2004.

Lu-In Wang, *Discrimination by Default: How Racism Becomes Routine*. New York: New York University Press, 2006.

Bernard E. Whitley and Mary E. Kite, *The Psychology of Prejudice and Discrimination*. Belmont, CA: Wadsworth, 2005.

Evan Wolfson, *Why Marriage Matters: America, Equality, and Gay People's Right to Marry*. New York: Simon & Schuster, 2004.

Periodicals

Moustafa Ayad, "Arab-American, Like Me," *Pittsburgh Post-Gazette*, July 20, 2005.

Robert Benne and Gerald McDermott, "Gay Unions Undermine Society," *Roanoke Times*, February 22, 2004.

Mark David Blum, "A Matter of Personal Freedom: What's Love Got to Do with State-Sanctioned Marriage?" *Post-Standard* (Syracuse, NY), December 2, 2004.

Liz Brody, "The Minority Report," *O, the Oprah Magazine*, April 2005.

Victoria A. Brownworth, "Civil Disobedience—Civil Rights," *Curve*, vol. 14, no. 4, June 2004.

Pamela Burdman, "Making the Case for Affirmative Action," *Black Issues in Higher Education*, June 2, 2005.

Rosalinda De Jesus-Staples, "By Any Means Necessary," *Hispanic Outlook in Higher Education*, Sept. 26, 2005.

Kevin Duchschere, "Is Gay Marriage a Civil-Rights Issue? Five Black Leaders Say It's Not Same," *Star Tribune* (Minneapolis, MN), March 26, 2004.

Economist, "The Case for Gay Marriage," February 28, 2004.

———, "The Forgotten Underclass: Poor Whites," October 28, 2006.

Sarwat Husain, "Law and Media See Muslims as Criminals, Fuel More Hate," *San Antonio Express-News*, September 19, 2003.

Hussein Ibish, "Let's Not Spite Our Face with Profiling," Progressive Muslim Union, 2005. www.pmuna.org/archives/2005/08/pmu_speaks_out.php.

Raina Kelley, "Let's Talk About Race; in the Aftermath of Michael Richards's Meltdown at the Laugh Factory, It's Time to Tell the Truth About What's Too Scary to Say Out Loud," *Newsweek*, December 4, 2006.

Rod Liddle, "Black People Are Shooting Each Other Because We Treat Them as a 'Community,'" *Spectator*, February 24, 2007.

David Limbaugh, "'Gay Marriage' Is Not About 'Rights,'" *Jewish World Review*, February 27, 2004. www.jewishworldreview.com/david/limbaugh022704.asp.

Michelle Malkin, "Racial Profiling: A Matter of Survival," *USA Today*, August 17, 2004. www.usatoday.com/news/opinion/editorials/2004-08-16-racial-profiling_x.htm.

Howard Manly, "Gay vs. Civil Rights Fight Misses Point," *Boston Herald*, March 9, 2004.

John McWhorter, "'Racism!' They Charged: When Don't They?" *National Review*, September 26, 2005.

Julissa Reynoso, "My Name Is Not Julie: When I Least Expected It, Racism Ruined the Party," *Colorlines Magazine*, Winter 2005.

William Rusher, "Let the States Decide What 'Marriage' Is," *WorldNetDaily.com*, March 4, 2004.

Steven Salaita, "The New Civilian Terrorists: Anti-Arab Racism Shapes the U.S. Discussion of the Middle East," *Colorlines Magazine*, January/February 2007.

Richard H. Sander, "Affirmative Action Hurts Those It's Supposed to Help," *Pittsburgh Tribune-Review*, January 2, 2005. www.pittsburghlive.com/x/pittsburghtrib/s_288430.html.

Thomas Tryon, "Conservative Arguments Compel Support for Gay Marriage," *Sarasota Herald Tribune*, March 14, 2004.

Graham Wagstaff, "Understanding Prejudice," *Psychology Review*, April 2005.

Walter Williams, "Racial Profiling," *Jewish World Review*, December 20, 2006. http://jewishworldreview.com/cols/williams122006.php3.

Web Sites

American Association for Affirmative Action (www.affirmative action.org). A national association of professionals seeking to promote understanding and advocacy of affirmative action to enhance access and equality in employment, economic, and educational opportunities.

American Muslim Council (www.amcnational.org). Founded in 1990, this organization seeks to increase the political participation of Muslim Americans. The Web site has the group's history, current projects, news releases, and links to more than three dozen other Islamic Web sites.

Asian Nation (www.asian-nation.org). An excellent information resource and overview of the historical, demographic, political, and cultural issues that make up today's Asian American community.

The Black Commentator (www.blackcommentator.com). A Web site published for an African American audience. Contains numerous cartoons, articles, essays, and links to other resources about contemporary issues facing African Americans.

Council on American Islamic Relations (www.cair-net.org). A nonprofit organization that works with journalists and others to improve the image of Islam and Muslims. The Web site contains news releases, action alerts, and information on how the media portray Islam.

Hate Crimes Research Network (www.hatecrime.net). Based out of Portland State University in Oregon, the HCRN links work done by sociologists, criminologists, psychologists, and others on the topic of hate crimes. The goal is to create a common pool of research and data to understand the phenomenon of hate crimes.

Hispanic Online (www.hispaniconline.com). A site containing a wealth of information related to the Hispanic community.

National Organization for Women (www.now.org). The National Organization for Women (NOW) is the largest organization of feminist activists in the United States. NOW works to eliminate discrimination and harassment in the workplace, schools, the justice system, and all other sectors of society; secure abortion, birth control, and reproductive rights for all women; end all forms of violence against women; eradicate racism, sexism, and homophobia; and promote equality and justice in society.

Race Watch (www.zmag.org/racewatch/racewatch.cfm). An enormous collection of articles on racism and discrimination provided by ZNet, an online library of social issues.

INDEX

PICTURE CREDITS